W9-BCJ-356

HEART FULL OF SOUL

An Inspirational Memoir

About Finding Your Voice

and Finding Your Way

Crown Publishers New York

HEART FULL OF SOUL

TAYLOR HICKS

with David Wild

Published in the United States by Crown Publishers,
an imprint of the Crown Publishing Group,
a division of Random House, Inc., New York.
www.crownpublishing.com

Crown is a trademark and the Crown colophon is a
registered trademark of Random House, Inc.

Library of Congress Cataloging-in-Publication Data
Hicks, Taylor, 1976–
    Heart full of soul : an inspirational memoir about finding
your voice and finding your way / Taylor Hicks.—1st ed.
      p. cm.
    Includes index.
    1. Hicks, Taylor, 1976–   2. Singers—United States—
Biography. I. Title.
    ML420.H396A3   2007
    782.42164092—dc22
    [B]   2007013373

ISBN 978-0-307-38243-6

Printed in the United States of America

DESIGN BY BARBARA STURMAN

10 9 8 7 6 5 4 3 2 1

First Edition

What is soul? It's like electricity—we don't really know
what it is, but it's a force that can light a room.

—RAY CHARLES

Contents

1
THE GRAY-HAIRED
BOY IN THE BUBBLE

YOU TAKE A TRIP TO THE CITY LIGHTS
AND TAKE THE LONG WAY HOME

—"Take the Long Way Home" by Rick Davies and
Roger Hodgson

For the better part of a year, I'd been living inside a bubble called *American Idol.* While the rest of the world could look in and see me, the fact is, from where I stood stage right at the Kodak Theater in Hollywood, California, on the evening of May 24, 2006, it was nearly impossible to see out. There I was, the gray-haired boy in the bubble, living out a strange but often thrilling version of the American dream in comfortable isolation.

In the exciting and exhausting weeks building up to the *Idol* finale, I'd get occasional calls from friends and family reporting on what was going on in the outside world. Still, I felt incredibly cut off—both physically and emotionally. Being at the center of the most-watched reality show in history turned out *not* to be the best vantage point from which to appreciate how big it all was. I knew this much, though: tonight—one way or another, win or lose—the bubble I was living in would burst in a very big and public way.

All around me backstage at the Kodak—the same fancy venue where the *real* Hollywood stars gathered each year for the Oscars—there was a sort of focused commotion playing out. From producers to stagehands, the folks who put together *American Idol* were all experienced pros, proud veterans of show business wars, but even they seemed to be feeling the full heat of the spectacle. As I took in the scene, I saw the clocks counting down, signaling just minutes left before the much-hyped 2006 finale of *American Idol* would begin.

Standing near me was Ryan Seacrest—a good guy who appears to have been genetically engineered to stand in the TV and radio spotlight. The man is a broadcasting machine who never stops working. At that moment, Ryan was busy getting his makeup touched up so he'd be ready to take the stage and direct traffic on what had become the biggest show on earth.

Tonight there'd definitely be heavy—and glamorous—congestion with all sorts of superstars on hand to take part in the *Idol* festivities. Amazingly, music greats Prince, Burt Bacharach, Dionne Warwick, Toni Braxton, Al Jarreau, and Meat Loaf were all here, as were Season 4 *American Idol* winner Carrie Underwood and the original Top 12 contestants from our season. Prince was keeping a low profile, though. Our surprise guest was hiding in his limo out back behind the Kodak Theater, where he'd stay until it was time for him to take the stage at night's end. To all of us producing and competing on the show, Prince was just this cool silhouette—a mysterious ghost of pure soulfulness.

Meat Loaf, on the other hand, was standing right there in the thick of things looking *exactly* like you'd imagine Meat Loaf to look—big, bold, and more than a little wild-eyed. Toni Braxton—with whom I'd be singing the Elvis Presley classic "In the Ghetto" later in the show—looked lovely, and couldn't have been nicer. Toni was even kind enough to bring me a gift she thought would be perfect for this moment in my life, a money clip.

"Taylor, I got you a money clip because you're going to *need* it," Toni said sweetly. "You're going to have a *lot* of money to fill this with." Of course, I was way too embarrassed to tell her that, right then, all I had to fill that clip was a bunch of five- and ten-dollar bills—and a pretty *small* bunch at that. Believe me, you don't get rich being on reality TV unless you win—and maybe not even then. Still, I appreciated Toni's thoughtfulness and optimism.

Stars weren't just lining up to be *on* the show tonight—we even had stars joining the audience, hooked on the excitement just like everyone else. For instance, the world's most beloved lifeguard, David Hasselhoff, was out front, as were a couple thousand other folks including my dad, Brad Hicks, his second wife, Linda, and my younger half brother, Sean. Our three famous judges—Paula Abdul, Randy Jackson, and Simon Cowell, who might best be described as infamous—

were also taking their places, attracting cheers and occasional catcalls from the crowd. Seemingly everywhere were executive producers Nigel Lythgoe and Ken Warwick, whose jobs, I'd come to learn, were as vague and ever-changing as they were important.

Debbie Williams—one of our stage managers, a little woman with a big personality who early on helped me figure out how to play to a TV camera the way I played to audiences in southern clubs and roadhouses—came over to tell me some breaking news. Debbie let me know that we'd have to rehearse one of the numbers during a commercial break. We'd simply run out of time to rehearse all the numbers in this two-hour show. That's just the way things sometimes went on *Idol*. We were all doing *so* much—and doing it *so* quickly—that we were continually in danger of falling behind.

Even during the show's quieter moments—and there *weren't* all that many—being on *American Idol* felt like riding some crazy bullet train. The problem was, you were never sure if you'd get thrown off the train. That's the thing about reality TV—it offers a unique crash course in fame, one that can end suddenly and painfully. As you might imagine, the whole experience can be thrilling, exciting, and a little scary—a real trip in every sense of the word.

Somehow, to the surprise of a whole lot of naysayers—the sort I'd been facing most of my life—I'd actually made it to this final destination, the Big Show, the *Idol* finale. In the end, it had all come down to just Katharine McPhee and myself. The two of us didn't talk much to each other as we awaited the big decision that evening. It was nothing personal, though. Truth be told, I'd been living inside my head most of the show, and possibly most of my life. I liked Katharine and knew that she'd worked hard to get this far. Plus, let's face it, she was pretty easy on the eyes, and it was more fun looking at her than Chris Daughtry.

Before the finale, we were both being held in the costume change rooms just off the side of the stage—positioned there so that the stage managers didn't have to run too far to get us into position. For our first appearance of the night, we were wearing white—*not* exactly my favorite color. I guess I've never felt innocent enough to pull it off, plus I already have hair that color.

As the seconds ticked away, I thought about everything that had led to this big moment. I was proud that I'd played the *American Idol* game so well, that my strategy had paid off—so far, at least. From the beginning my main focus was turning my biggest disadvantage into an advantage. The undeniable truth is that by nearly every standard, I didn't fit in. I was older and fatter, and I had gray hair. So I decided the smart thing to do was embrace my oddness for all it was worth—like they say, *vive la différence.*

People who worked on *Idol* tell me that I stood out from the beginning as someone who was thinking ahead. Early in the competition, when I was discussing a particular performance with our show director, Bruce Gowers, and Debbie, they asked if I wanted to go out into the audience during the number. I told them I was saving that move for later in the series. Much later, they'd tell me they were shocked by my display of confidence. They realized I was thinking weeks down the line, while the other contestants were all just trying to survive week to week.

Another time Debbie kidded me about my gut, which, unfortunately, had gotten more noticeable during all those weeks with easy access to free catering tables. "Watch out, Taylor, you've got a little *belly* there," she said as nicely as those words can be said. I looked her straight in the eye and replied, "Hey, middle America *loves* that belly." And you know, I don't think I was too far off. America loved my belly more than Ace Young's six-pack. I understood middle America because *that's* where I'm from. That's who I *am*. I'm not from Sherman Oaks, California. I'm from Birmingham, Alabama, and that's as middle America as you can get—okay, perhaps not geographically, but in every other way.

As a guy whose hair began turning gray at fourteen, I was pretty used to standing out from the pack. For years, my many flaws held me back. But once I got on *American Idol* I began to see that not being perfect—or *looking* perfect—could pay off in a huge way. If America wanted flaws they could relate to, I had *plenty* to go around. And when the show was over and all the votes were counted, I figured there'd be plenty of time to work on that belly.

Standing there backstage waiting for the *Idol* finale to

begin, I wondered for a moment if I'd have to settle for second place. After years of struggle, though, I knew that getting the consolation prize wouldn't be enough. Deep down, I think I needed an undeniable sign that the crazy dream I'd chosen of making music was the right one. Winning would be that sign.

All I ever really wanted was to be recognized for making the soulful music that had saved me as a young man. I thought of my dad out in the crowd, sitting with his second wife and their son. We were all cool now, and I was glad to have them there. My mom had come to the show to watch once too. As I'll tell you about shortly, there were bumpy family histories all around me, but it was still good to see my dad there. At long last, he was getting confirmation that I wasn't the good-for-nothing bum he worried I might become.

Like a lot of people, I didn't grow up in the kind of happy family featured in TV sitcoms. My family started falling apart when I was just a little kid, and in many ways it never really came back together. When I was young, I learned a lot of things the hard way. For one thing, I learned that alcohol and family are a horrible and explosive combination. And as I grew up in the middle of chaos and bad behavior, I also learned that nothing is guaranteed—not even a normal childhood.

Winning the *American Idol* title and taking home that dream record deal with Clive Davis and J Records would be the closest thing to a guarantee this boy from Birmingham,

Alabama, would ever get. But first I had to be judged, and not just by Randy, Paula, and Simon. I had to be judged by America.

In truth, I'd known my way around judges from a very early age. Way before getting on *Idol,* I'd been judged plenty— by family, by teachers, by myself, and even by an actual judge or two. The first time was when I was maybe five or six years old. I found myself in a hot Birmingham courtroom facing a judge whose job it was to decide whether I'd be better off living with my mom or my dad. For a few years, I'd been bouncing around with my mom, who was bouncing all over the place herself—in *many* ways. I still remember how, right in front of everyone, the judge asked me in a thick Alabama accent, "So, *son,* does your mother drink?" What could I say? For the record, here's what I *did* say: "Yes, sir, she *sure* does."

Suddenly, the whole courtroom lit up in laughter. All those grown-ups looking at me just about *died.* Now, in retrospect, I know it really wasn't all that inspired a punch line. I guess it was funny because it was *true.* And so it was that I gave up the goods on my mother and a shameless new entertainer was born.

Anyway, having been judged so much along the way, as a kid and then later as a never-give-up road warrior trying to catch a break, I knew that in the end you *can't* really sing to a whole country—that's just not how it works. And unless you happen to be Ray Charles, nobody has a voice that can force tens of millions to believe in you. That's not a trick anyone can play—least of all someone like me, a gray-haired bar singer from Birmingham.

To sing to the whole world, you've really got to do it one person at a time—at least, that's how it feels for me. That's what a lost decade spent playing lousy gigs and tough rooms has taught me. Singing from your soul isn't about how many notes you can hit or how long you can hold them. It's all about intimacy and honesty. It's about sharing your story in a song—whether it happens to be a song you wrote or one you decided to make your own.

The only job I ever really wanted comes down to looking somebody in the eyes and telling them the truth—telling them *my* truth. Music has given me almost everything that's good in my life. Mother music, I call it. When something gives you so much, you damn well better give back everything you can in return. If you're going to dare to pick up that microphone, you better have something to say, something to share.

So I guess that's what I did the night of the finale—tried to share.

Later, after it was over, I remember thinking—with disbelief—that for about forty-five minutes there I was maybe the biggest star in the world. As Ryan would eventually announce, 63.4 million votes were cast for me that night—more than had been cast for the president of the United States only a year earlier.

But that was *later.*

As I walked onto the Kodak stage that night with a heart full of soul and took my place in the spotlight, it wasn't nerves I was feeling, but something else entirely. In truth, I felt right at home—a man in the right place at the right time. What was once a bubble had somehow become home—and really, home was what I'd been looking for all along.

2
CRYING TIME

SOMETIMES WE GET WEARY
AND FIND OURSELVES ALONE
IN A WORLD FULL OF DARKNESS
FOR THOSE WHO HAVE NO HOME.

—"Heart and Soul" by Taylor Hicks

My first memory is picture-perfect—like a postcard I wish someone had sent me.

It was Christmastime, and I remember that my mother and I were visiting for the holidays with my aunt Katherine and uncle Dan at their farm in Cullman, Alabama. At the time I must have been four years old. Aunt Katherine and Uncle Dan were family on my mother's side, and they lived out in the country in a big old white farmhouse. The place was peaceful and welcoming, surrounded by a pretty peach orchard and more cattle than I'd ever seen before.

My mom's side of the family had all gathered at the farm for Christmas that year. A great idea, because that December the farm had the look of a real-life winter wonderland. Strangely, though, it's not our Christmas morning I vividly recall—or whatever presents Santa happened to leave under the tree.

Instead, the thing I'll never forget is the complete thrill of searching for our family Christmas tree a few days earlier. The air was frigid that day and the snow was falling gently and quietly. I recall my mother bundling me up in a winter coat. Then—along with the rest of the family—the two of us went running out into all that snow. I remember how thrilling it felt to be heading off into the gorgeous frozen pine forest, which was now totally draped in white—all of us in hot pursuit of the same thing, the absolutely perfect tree.

At that point my idyllic memory gets a little snowy. I know we found a great tree, and I'm sure I loved whatever presents I found underneath it a few days later, but it's the memory of our wintry search that warms me even now. I wish I had *more* memories like that.

Just a few years after that Christmas, another holiday scene unfolded—one containing far less comfort and joy.

This time some of the same family members were gathered under far less perfect circumstances at another relative's house much closer to the city. It was an unusually warm Thanksgiving Day and I was still living with my mom, but by now I was a little older and there was trouble in the air.

My mother's father was a justice of the peace in the area, and as the food was being served he burst into the living room with his badge in his hand, thoroughly convinced that one of the Thanksgiving guests was a wanted man. A struggle broke out right there, and suddenly there was a loaded gun flying freely above our Thanksgiving meal.

Today, I can joke that I was simply overjoyed the gun didn't land in the turkey and discharge its bullets into the stuffing, but that really wasn't how I felt that day. For a few chilling seconds, I thought I'd lost my mind.

Somewhere between those two early memories, that's where you'll find my childhood.

In other words, it was the best of times. It was the worst of times.

As far as most people are concerned, Taylor Hicks was born in prime time on the Fox Broadcasting Company sometime during January 2006. My real story begins, though, a long time before that, on October 7, 1976, at Saint Vincent's Hospital in Birmingham, Alabama, where I entered the world as Taylor Reuben Hicks, the first—and, as things would pan out, *only*—child of Bradley and Pamela Hicks. I'm told I was big and loud, with an impressive shock of blond hair. But like so much else in my life, my hair color would change soon enough.

Bradley Hicks and Pamela Dickinson—the two people who'd become my parents—had first met back in high school in Birmingham, Alabama, sometime in the late sixties. No record remains of what kind of sparks flew at their initial moment of contact. Yet, based on the undeniable fact of my existence, there must have been at least a brief moment when the two got along—or at the very least got together.

All these years later, neither my mother nor father is inclined to discuss their years as a couple, but after my conception there must have been *some* occasional happiness.

Unfortunately, by the time I was old enough to really reflect on how my parents got along, their marriage was already in the long, painful, and sometimes ugly process of falling totally apart. When I close my eyes now and try to picture Mom and Dad together, I only see vague images of two people in conflict—sometimes horrible conflict.

The experts say that opposites attract, and if they're right, there must have been a tremendous attraction going on in the beginning, because by the time I came to know my parents—in all their glory and displaying all their very human faults—they were two extremes already headed in opposite directions.

My mother was—and is—a uniquely beautiful lady, tall with dark brown hair and the most piercing crystal blues eyes you can imagine. She's always had an exotic, vaguely bohemian look all her own. She stood out in Birmingham, Alabama. Hell, she stood out *anywhere.* Over the years, many people have told me I look just like my mother, and I suppose I should take that as a compliment.

Then and now, when the mood strikes, my mom can be the most charming and entertaining person on earth. With her great smile and carefree spirit, she sometimes acts more like a fun older sister than a typical mother. But like a lot of highly entertaining people, concentrating on life's routine but important tasks is not her strength.

After my parents split up when I was four, I initially went to live with my mom. Subsequently, the two of us moved a lot, cramming into a bunch of tiny apartments and constantly driving around in her old Honda Civic hatchback. For a time, we settled—in so much as we ever *settled*—in Huntsville, Alabama.

Mom worked at different jobs along the way, including being a receptionist and a medical transcriptionist—pretty much anything ending with an "-ist." Moving around as much as I did, I came to learn quite quickly how to make new friends. At the same time, I knew to keep some distance and even some secrets.

More than any of the places we temporarily called home, what I remember most clearly from those years is the feeling of being in constant motion. While driving around with my mom, listening to the radio always made things a little better. And I guess that's when I tried out singing for the first time— trucking down the highways and the country roads of Alabama screaming along to "When Doves Cry" by Prince, never even dreaming that someday I'd share the stage with the man himself.

So many of my memories of growing up around my mom involve being in a car with her, and that seems fitting because it often felt as if we were headed somewhere we could never quite reach. Life could be a blast with Mom, but it rarely felt settled or safe.

Sometimes we could laugh about it. One time when I was about seven, Mom borrowed a car and my aunt told her to be careful because this particular Datsun had the shimmies. We didn't really know what my aunt meant by that, but we both agreed the word *shimmies* was hilarious. At least, it seemed hilarious until the car hit forty-five miles an hour and the damn thing nearly fell apart in the middle of the road. I remember being terrified that the brakes would shimmy right off the car, and yet still laughing because my mom was laughing the whole time.

I loved that my mother could be so carefree and entertaining. There were other times I'd rather forget—disturbing memories of being a little kid cooking on a hot stove and thinking, *Something is wrong here.* Like that Datsun with the shimmies, my mom was sometimes just all over the place.

My father was, as I've said, kind of Mom's opposite. A good-looking guy in his own right, he differed from Mom in that he was straighter, quieter, and more intense.

By nature or nurture, my dad seemed to pick up all those stray cares my mother refused to worry about. While the Dickinson side of my family clearly knew how to have fun— a bit *too* much at times—the Hicks side was defined by a much more serious work ethic and view of life. By a process of parental elimination, my dad was—or simply had to become—the more responsible party. My father was—and remains to this day—a quiet man whose approach to the world is, "Walk softly and carry a big stick." And if you lived with him, as I eventually did most of the time, Dad never let you forget that big stick.

To his eternal credit, though, my dad was *there*. Even when my mother had custody of me, my father drove two hours on the weekend just to see how I was doing. Things may not have always been easy when he arrived, especially with support checks changing hands along with yours truly, but he always showed up wherever we were so he could make sure I was okay. It would be many years before I'd understand that this wasn't something every divorced dad cared enough to do.

I think I knew on some level that my dad cared a lot about me. Looking back, I felt closest to him when we'd spend Saturdays together watching Alabama football games. In Alabama, watching college football is like a religion, only louder, and the Hicks family worshiped with great gusto on countless weekends. We were never great at expressing feelings, but put a big game on TV and the emotional floodgates opened. We'd hug and slap hands when our team won, and we'd be in tears and full gridiron mourning after a loss. My dad *loved* Alabama football, and at times like that, I believed he loved me too.

For much of my childhood, my parents were very caught up in their own situations. Most of the time, their focus seemed less on me and more on trying to get away from each other before somebody got killed. My parents probably haven't said ten words to each other in the last ten years, and that seems to be working out just fine.

Looking back, most of my worst family memories resulted from coming face-to-face with the downside of alcohol. There's a history of alcoholism and drug abuse in my family. From an early age, I learned that there are two kinds of drunks—teddy-bear drunks and mean drunks. Suffice it to say that I've been around more of the latter. Booze and family are a volatile combination at best, and throughout my childhood various combinations kept exploding in my face. On my father's side, it was more a matter of Miller High Life. On my mother's, the brew was more complex.

To put it in perspective, it sometimes helps to think back to what was going on in the world at the end of the seventies and early eighties, when I was little. I realize that my parents were ultimately just two poorly matched people who were living through, and seeking to survive, those particular times. As a kid, things often got confusing, but now, with the passage of time, I can see that my parents were pretty hip cats who were grooving and shaking with the era. I'm not sure that either ever really understood me because they were too busy trying to figure themselves out.

It just so happened that my mother and father were coming of age during the time of sex, drugs, and rock and roll. They were two attractive young people stuck with a busted marriage and a little son in Alabama. They were living out the hard-partying era—not with all the beautiful people at Studio 54 in New York City, but rather in their own down-home southern way.

For better or worse, those were much freer times, and in the end all three of us paid a price for that freedom.

After my star turn in court when my father was finally awarded custody of me, I moved into the apartment he shared with his second wife, Linda, in Hoover, Alabama—a suburb of Birmingham. At first, my new circumstances seemed promising. As the only child of an utterly broken marriage, I was excited to be moving into a nicer apartment with my dad, a new potential mother figure in Linda, a younger stepbrother named Jeremy, whose room I now invaded, and even my very own little half brother, named Sean.

Somehow, though, things didn't pan out exactly as we hoped. That perfect comfort zone I imagined as a kid never quite emerged. I'm sure that blending families can be a very beautiful thing, but take it from me, it can be awfully hard to find that perfect blend.

Fortunately, these days we're all on much better terms with one another. Now we really *are* a kind of family, but at the time I often felt like I was in the way—a not entirely welcome reminder of a past mistake. I couldn't help feeling that

I'd upset the apple cart just as my dad and Linda were trying to start their own family. I felt like the odd man out, a role I'd get to play many times in the years to come.

When thing got too tense in our apartment, I'd just go elsewhere and wait it out. In particular, my dad's parents—my grandmother Jonie and my grandfather Earl, who lived nearby—did their best to look after me. I believe my grandmother Jonie saw what was going on and tried to mother me as much as she could.

People often ask me if I come from a musical family, and the truth is, I really don't. There was a little bluegrass on my mother's side, and I do remember my grandmother Jonie singing "Old Rugged Cross" to me a few times. She wasn't exactly Mahalia Jackson or even Amy Grant, but she could carry a tune.

I wish her cooking was as adept. It can be difficult to find a truly bad cook in the South, but I never had a problem whenever my grandmother was around. Please understand, I love that woman with all my heart, but the truth is, Jonie Hicks made meatloaf that just about glowed in the dark. Even though there was no gunplay, her Thanksgiving dinners were like culinary horror movies, and we were all the victims. Literally, there were times when you'd find pieces of old Campbell Soup labels mixed in the gravy. One time I remember my father biting into his food and discovering a plastic bread tie. My grandfather calmly told him to be quiet and put the tie back on the bread where it belonged. My grandmother has been a true guiding light, but she also taught me to appreciate eating in restaurants.

In his own very low-key way, my grandfather Earl also tried his best to keep me out of harm's way while still letting me do my thing. I always sensed that he got a kick out of me, which was nice for a change. In the Hicks family *everybody* worked, which gave me plenty of time to get into trouble. My grandfather went to work every weekday morning for thirty-five years at the American Cast Iron Pipe Company in Birmingham, Alabama.

For my seventh birthday, Grandpa used his connections there to have a dump truck load of sand dropped in the woods behind our house. Here I was, a kid who dreamed of having a sandbox, and instead I got this huge load of sand brought straight to me by an actual truck. I was in heaven.

Unfortunately, I was by then turning into a juvenile pyromaniac, lighting up leaves and almost anything else I could get my hands on. So what did I do with this wonderful gift from my grandfather? Basically, I used that ten-foot pile of sand to put out as many fires as I could possibly start.

I'll never forget the day when I almost killed myself and someone else with my red-hot stupidity. It was a hot and windy Alabama afternoon, and I managed to talk a female playmate into joining me for a little fire starting. After I got the thing going, it hit me that I'd forgotten to put any sand in my pail. I'm sorry to say that I almost burned myself and that little girl that day. Fortunately, someone spotted the potential inferno and immediately called the fire department. As the firemen rushed to save the neighborhood, I realized an invaluable if obvious life lesson: *Don't start any fires you can't put out.*

Looking back, it seems that most of my lessons were self-taught. I even learned table manners—or failed to do so—on my own. As a result, you could say I still have an approach to dining room etiquette that is, at best, unorthodox. With music, I suppose it was pretty much the same messy approach. I didn't learn how to make music the *right* way—I learned how to do it *my* way. Sometimes ignorance really *is* bliss, at least if you're the ignorant one. And in the end, eating and making music remain two things I really love to do. They're my two favorite forms of daily sustenance.

I wish we'd had the money to eat out more. The Hicks side of my family had more resources than the Dickinson side, but neither was what you might call fully loaded. Even though my father was a dentist, money could be a problem. My dad had a small practice locally, and he often drove throughout the area, scrounging enough business to support us all. Through the good times and the not-so-good times, Dad kept working hard no matter what.

As a kid, I spent many hours goofing around in Dad's office. I remember making fillings, fooling with the nitrous oxide, and my favorite activity, throwing mercury on the floor and watching it divide into a million pieces only to come back together again. At times, I could actually be productive, helping Dad to fill a tooth. But mostly, I exhibited way too much energy.

When it came to getting dental work from my dad, it seemed that I was plagued by bad luck. I remember getting my two teeth knocked out during the final game of my only moderately distinguished high school basketball career. I went up for an important shot in the closing minutes and came back down with two fewer teeth. I rushed home and got my teeth fixed by my dad—free of charge, of course. Two days later, though, while fishing, I cast out my line and heard something extra plop into the water—my two teeth.

A couple days later, after Dad had put the bonding back in, I was inhaling breakfast at a nearby Waffle House when my teeth fell out again, leaving me looking a little like the Jim Carrey character in *Dumb and Dumber,* only dumber. For the first time in my life, I thought, *Maybe I should find another dentist.*

Where we lived, at least, Christmas was a particularly rough time in the dentistry business. Nobody loves the dentist, especially not around holiday season. Who wants to get a tooth pulled and end up missing their fancy dinner? As a result, toward year's end, it always seemed like money was a little tight.

But our seasonal slowdowns taught me about the value of hard work. When the demand for tooth pulling dried up during the holidays, my grandmother—who worked at the big shopping mall in town—arranged for Dad to become the photographer for the mall's singing Santa.

Grandma actually had a truly inspired marketing mind. And I like to think that I've inherited a little of her savvy. After all, if I can successfully market myself with all my flaws, I must be a damn fine salesman, right? Grandma's job was to do whatever it took to get people to come into the mall to shop. Over the years, she came up with some very original ideas for drawing a crowd. One time, she arranged to have thousands of numbered Ping-Pong balls dropped out of a small airplane. Each of the balls corresponded to an inexpensive gift the recipient could collect from one of the mall's many stores.

Initially, the idea looked like a massive hit. The day of the big ball drop there must have been ten thousand people out there in that Alabama field waiting for Ping-Pong balls to land on their heads.

Unfortunately, some unusually strong winds were blowing, and they managed to turn Grandma's tiny brainstorm into a gigantic mess that people in the Birmingham area still talk about. Most of the windblown balls landed all over the nearby interstate, spurring ten thousand people to risk life and limb snatching them from in front of oncoming cars.

If you ever hear that I'm air-dropping copies of one of my CDs, you'll understand that such grand and crazy schemes run in the Hicks family. In all honesty, I thoroughly respect my grandmother's ability to dream big. It's probably from Grandma that I got my desire—and ability—to draw a crowd.

But back then, I still didn't have a clue as to what skill I might develop to get people to gather round.

3
UNCHAIN MY HEART

I'VE BEEN TRAVELING ALL THESE YEARS,

JUST BARELY GETTING BY.

THE ROAD CAN BE YOUR FRIEND

OR THE DEVIL IN DISGUISE

WHEN THE TOUGH GET GOING

THE MUSES VISIT ME

YET IN SLOW, LOW TONES, THEY ALWAYS SAY TO ME

SAY TO ME

IT AIN'T NO GROOVE THING

IT AIN'T NO COUNTRY TWANG

IT'S A SIMPLE REFRAIN

IT'S A SOUL THING.

—"Soul Thing" by Taylor Hicks

P lease don't wake up the kids to tell them this, but every once in a while, crime really *does* pay.

Growing up, I was a very occasional—and thoroughly second-rate—shoplifter. I do hereby confess to acquiring some Winston Red cigarettes and at least a few issues of *Playboy* under highly questionable circumstances. But if there's such a thing as the perfect crime of passion, mine occurred one auspicious afternoon when I wrongly—and yet somehow still righteously—stole a dusty old copy of *The Best of Otis Redding* from my friend Greg Garnette's home.

I must have been in fourth grade at the time, so in my defense, this criminal act did take place just as my family was experiencing particularly rough times. One day after school I was over at Greg's house. I did that a lot in those days—hang out at other kids' houses. When your own home is in turmoil, you look for anyplace you can walk or run to that feels welcome and safe.

Looking back now, I'm sure there were days and nights when I overstayed my welcome—my buddy Lee Collier, for example, saw a *whole lot* of me. But like some southern-fried version of Eddie Haskell on *Leave It to Beaver*, I had the gift of gab and usually did my best to ingratiate myself with my friends' parents. For me, this wasn't just ass-kissing. I genuinely loved hanging out with many of them, either because I was an old soul or a young kid in pain. Maybe a little of both.

Fortunately for me, on that day I was hanging with Greg I noticed that his parents owned an extremely cool record collection full of classic soulful oldies. By this time, I was singing along to oldies radio every chance I got, as well as the pop-rock favored by kids my own age. I have no idea whether I sang well, but I sang with all my heart. Prior to that afternoon, it's entirely possible I'd heard Otis Redding singing "(Sittin' On) The Dock of the Bay" on the radio. But if I had, I hadn't appreciated its full, funky force. That was about to change.

I remember sitting there in the Garnettes' sunny living room with my mouth open, just staring at the album's tattered old cover and listening intently over and over again to these stunning songs unfold: "I've Been Loving You Too Long (to Stop Now)," "These Arms of Mine," "I Can't Turn You Loose," "A Change Is Gonna Come," and the original, pre–Aretha Franklin version of "Respect."

Song after song blew my young mind. For a time I think I forgot entirely about my friend Greg, and even about being there in his house. The music spoke to me and yet took me outside of myself. As I hung on every word and every note Otis delivered, it felt as if I'd become unstuck in time. It was as if I'd found the mysterious but instantly relatable music that had always been within my own divided soul. Listening to Otis work his magic that day, a whole new soulful world opened up.

In a flash, I became a willing new student of this remarkable American music. Suddenly, my young life had some slight, soulful sense of direction. In the weeks and months that followed, I started gathering as many records as I could. Some were by artists slightly closer to my own generation, such as Van Morrison, Steely Dan, and Supertramp. But I soon began moving rapidly backward through music history. Most of all, I became obsessed with sweet soul music, which spoke directly to me.

I began haunting the record shop at the Galleria—the biggest mall in Birmingham—in search of knowledge. Soon I learned that much of the music that moved me had been made in the American South, just like me. I read that Otis Redding had been working as a bus driver for a blues guitarist named Johnny Jenkins when he stepped up to the microphone at Stax Studio in Memphis, Tennessee, and became an overnight sensation. I discovered that only a few short busy years later, in 1967, Otis had died tragically in a plane crash at the age of twenty-six. Fortunately, before he left life's stage, he'd already established himself as a towering figure in the history of deep soul music, leaving behind a legacy that would live forever.

Reading through the album credits that afternoon at Greg's house, I noticed that Otis Redding had written or co-written many of the songs himself. My English teachers typically had trouble getting me interested in, say, Mark Twain, but suddenly, who wrote every soul song seemed very, very important to me.

One of the tracks that I noticed Otis did *not* write was his breathtaking version of "A Change Is Gonna Come." That tune had been written by someone named Sam Cooke. Now I had someone else to seek out and discover.

Soon I'd learn that Sam Cooke was also long dead—but a little thing like life or death couldn't deter my interest. By any means necessary, I needed to know everything I could about these amazing individuals and the music they'd kindly left behind.

Yet at the moment I was listening to "A Change Is Gonna Come" all I really knew was that Otis Redding was digging deep, talking about having faith in troubled times. For me, it was a revelation. I hadn't known that music like this existed—music that spoke powerfully to life's pain and somehow made you feel better all at the same time. Do yourself a favor and listen closely to an Otis Redding song sometime—try "Fa-Fa-Fa-Fa-Fa (Sad Song)." I defy you *not* to feel better afterward.

That's the glorious, uplifting thing about truly soulful music. To borrow a phrase from John Mellencamp, even when soul music hurts, it hurts so good.

People who don't follow music much usually assume that blues music must be pretty depressing listening. Of course, the exact *opposite* has always been true. Nothing is more positive and ultimately more life-affirming than hearing a great singer work through pain and problems by singing to you straight from his or her heart.

Instantly, I knew that the music on this album was *my* music. Hearing Otis Redding sing stirred deep emotions, some that I didn't even know I had. Soul music is gospel music for *everyone*—black or white, sinner or saint—and it lifted me up like nothing before or since. This music didn't just touch my soul; I think perhaps it awakened it for the very first time.

Now, I wish I could say that this transcendent moment inspired me to greatness immediately. Unfortunately, it first inspired a petty crime. I remember feeling that I *had* to get this kind of music in my life right away. And so it was that, for arguably the best of reasons, I did the worst of things and secretly put the Garnettes' album in my book bag, praying silently that no one would notice my terrible sin. It was almost as if I hoped that by taking the album home, I'd be able to carry these new feelings with me wherever I went.

When I put the record on my own turntable, I couldn't stop singing along to another of its songs, "Try a Little Tenderness." The song killed me then just as it kills me now.

I guess I was looking for any tenderness I could find back then. A few days later, I sang the song for my grandmother Jonie, who was nice enough to at least *act* suitably impressed. That might have been one of my first good reviews—and maybe the most important, because that was probably the first time I thought of myself as a singer.

To this day, I still keep that old Otis Redding platter safely tucked away in storage for whenever I need it. And when, years after my crime, I guiltily confessed to Greg, he told me to just keep the album and not worry about it. Fortunately, my friend was wise enough to realize that, for whatever reason, I needed that album a whole lot more than he did.

Having finally been turned loose by the music of Otis Redding, I began in earnest to give myself a full-blown soul education. I started by studying such greats as Sam Cooke, James Brown, Sam and Dave, Aretha Franklin, and Marvin Gaye. And just so it's clear that I'm not a man of prejudice, let me assure you that I checked out some splendid *white* soul singers too, including Bob Seger, Steve Winwood, Joe Cocker, and the great Van "The Man" Morrison.

As I threw myself into my musical studies, I started to see the subtle and sometimes not so subtle connections between all these great American artists. I wanted to know where each had come from and where each had then traveled.

Eventually, I discovered that all roads lead back to one

man, who more than anyone else created the art form that had given me a new sense of purpose—the one and only Genius of Soul, Ray Charles. The first time I ever heard the singular sound of Ray Charles' singing I was in the record store at the mall. "I Can't Stop Lovin' You" came over the sound system, and immediately I was transfixed. For this soul-loving boy from Alabama, there it all was on one heartbreaking record: the source of the Nile.

By then I was ten and the closest thing to a real-life hero I had was Adrian Cronauer—the unorthodox and irreverent U.S. Armed Forces Radio DJ whom Robin Williams portrayed in *Good Morning, Vietnam.* Reflecting on it now, *Good Morning, Vietnam* seems an odd movie for a kid my age to identify with so strongly. Still, something about the idea of this solitary man trying with all his heart and soul to entertain people who were in a truly tough situation connected with me.

After that trip to the mall, I had a *new* hero, though— one I could interact with through his art. I listened to every Ray Charles track I could get my hands on, and this time I didn't steal the music. Listening to Ray was a privilege for which I was more than willing to pay.

For me, calling Brother Ray the "Genius of Soul" is too limiting considering that he made every song he sang his own—and that includes "America the Beautiful." I think Frank Sinatra—a guy who obviously knew a thing or two about singing—put it better when he once called Ray "the only true genius in the business."

By all accounts, Ray could be a tough man, but growing up the way he did, in the business he did and in the time he did, the man *had* to be tough to make it through. For me, his genius lies in his ability to take everything he was contending with—the good, the bad, and the ugly—and put it all right into his music.

But I admire much more than Ray's creative genius. Recently I was rereading Ray's autobiography, *Brother Ray*, for what's probably the hundredth time. In the book, he tells the story of how he had glaucoma as a child and began to lose his sight. And even *this* part of his story struck a chord with me. It dawned on me that during springtime in Alabama when I was a little kid, the pollen count would get so high that sometimes I'd have an allergic reaction and my eyes would become so jelled over that I couldn't see. I remember that, when this happened, my mother would call me "Lobster Boy" because I looked like something out of a cheesy horror movie.

Now, obviously I have absolutely no notion of what it's like to really go blind, any more than I know what it's like to be black in America. But for whatever reasons, everything about the pain and experience in Ray Charles' voice touched a raw nerve in me. I can feel not only the man's pain but also his strength and determination to endure and triumph against long odds. Whenever I find the going a little tough, I think about how hard life on the road must have been for Ray—this brilliant blind black man trying to find his way in an extremely racist world.

The music that's in my heart—soul music—taught me loudly and clearly that racism is nothing but pure ignorance. Soul music spoke to me—not because of the color of anybody's skin but because of the beauty and the power of its sound and the universal purity of its message. The music of Ray Charles—and the other soul greats I admire—is the music of healing, music that brings together people of all sorts.

One of the highlights of my career before *Idol* was the night I had the honor of opening up for the amazing Percy Sledge in Tuscaloosa, Alabama. After Percy sang his soul classics, including "When a Man Loves a Woman" and "Dark End of the Street," you could put a fork in me because I was pretty much done.

That night as I stood backstage I remember being struck that I was in the presence of a man who'd been singing some of the same songs for more than thirty years. Yet somehow he still sang them like he meant every word. Percy Sledge could do that because he *did* mean those songs. He understood that singing your heart out is not about what you get paid or how many people are watching you. Singing is about passing something on and connecting with whoever is out there in the dark watching.

One of the things I value most about the entire *American Idol* experience is the way the show allowed the contestants to turn on millions of kids to so much great music of the past. In an era of massive cutbacks in music education, we provided a little music education for people right there in prime time. I'll tell you, it makes me feel proud and honored every time a young kid comes up to me and asks about Otis Redding because I sang "Try a Little Tenderness" or about Sam Cooke because I performed "You Send Me." I feel like, whatever I received growing up, I now get to play some small role in passing it on.

So if you're young and reading these words and want to know what true soul really is, I urge you to take the time to study all the great soul singers—from Brother Ray Charles to Reverend Al Green to the queen of hip-hop soul, Mary J. Blige. Do yourself a favor and allow yourself to feel the inflection of emotion in their voices.

Now that I'd found my very worthy musical hero, I was ready not just to sing from the heart but to *blow* too. But it wasn't until I was sixteen that I finally made the great leap forward from being a major music fan to becoming an actual player myself.

I was hanging out with some friends at the flea market in Bessemer, Alabama, on a lazy Sunday afternoon when a beat-up old Marine Band harmonica suddenly caught my eye. That crusty old harp didn't just look used; it looked downright abused. Still, the price was definitely right, so after considerable debate, I dug into my pockets and made the single best $2 investment of my life. As for the *worst* $2 I've ever spent—well, that probably involved imbibing alcohol on some night I can no longer remember.

In what seemed like minutes, I fell totally and passionately in love with that harmonica. Right from the point I purchased it, that instrument and I became inseparable. The thing went to school with me. It went to bed with me. It even went to the bathroom with me. It kept me company and gave me a new identity. I was "the kid with the harmonica."

As I'd done with so much else in my life, I taught myself to play the instrument without any formal instruction. I took the harmonica straight to my records and began trying to play along with all my favorites. Whenever there was nobody around to yell at me to shut up, I played not just to soul and blues tunes but also to the rock tracks I loved by performers such as Eric Clapton, Bruce Springsteen, and Supertramp.

In particular, I spent many happy, productive days attempting to play along to Clapton's popular *Unplugged* album. There were a lot of great songs on that one in the key of G, and I was lucky enough to have the C harmonica, so that worked out just fine. But for me, the ultimate test was playing along to "Take the Long Way Home" by Supertramp. Day by day, month by month, I tried my best to keep up until I finally started to get, well . . . okay. I knew I was getting somewhere the day my father heard me playing along to "Take the Long Way Home" and actually stopped to listen. "Not *bad*, Taylor," he said. "Not bad at all."

4
SWEET HOME
ALABAMA

SWEET HOME ALABAMA

WHERE THE SKIES ARE SO BLUE

—"Sweet Home Alabama" by Ed King, Gary Rossington,
and Ronnie Van Zant

The first monumentally stupid act that I can remember committing back in my school days ended with me getting firmly paddled on the behind. Yet somehow I still came out singing in the end.

I was living with my mother at the time in Huntsville, Alabama, and going to second grade at Whitesburg Elementary School. For some strange reason, my little buddies and I devised a horrifying if oddly inventive game.

Though I can hardly believe it myself, here is how our sadistic youthful activity worked. One of our little group—we'd all take turns—would stand up against a wall in the school bathroom. Next we'd order the man—make that *boy*—of the hour to breathe as hard and fast as he possibly could. Then at the precise moment of the chosen one's heaviest and most rapid breathing, we'd all at once push on his chest so that the collective force of our body pressure would cut off the blood to his brain. At least for a moment.

Why exactly—you might reasonably ask—did a bunch of otherwise normal second graders all choose to freely participate in this highly reckless behavior that suggests some pip-squeak version of the movie *Fight Club*? Even now all these years later I really can't tell you, other than to simply state the obvious: we sure must have been a bunch of idiots.

One day, my own turn came to face this frightening bathroom challenge. Being the total moron I clearly must have been then, I recall doing exactly what I was supposed to do in keeping with the rules of our game.

Seeing as I was already a tad taller than the other guys in my second-grade gang—and quite possibly a little more annoying—my pals may have pushed on my chest a little harder than they had with previous "contestants." Anyway, disaster followed. I ended up passing out cold, falling hard toward the ground, and hitting my big head on a nearby toilet stall.

After that, the next thing I can remember is finding myself flat out on the school bathroom's cold tile floor with a huge black eye and a world of hurt all over my body. After my friends hailed a teacher, I was immediately rushed to the school nurse, who confirmed I'd live. Then came the worst part: visiting the principal so she could render judgment. There was little hemming and hawing. To her, the situation clearly called for paddling.

Now, clearly I had a vested interest here, but paddling my ass struck me as a somewhat redundant punishment. I was, after all, a kid who'd just been knocked very hard on that selfsame ass. Fortunately, Principal Paddle—I've forgotten her real name—administered her blows to me in an entirely humane style. Truth be told, she was pretty sweet about it.

Anyway, the reason I bring up Principal Paddle is that she often referred to our school's student body as the "Star-Spangled Singers" because it was her habit to go around the school spontaneously asking the kids to sing "My Country 'tis of Thee." And wouldn't you know it, not long after my bathroom episode, our patriotic principal asked me to belt out this great American standard. Apparently, my performance made an impression, because she subsequently selected me as one of the ten best singers in the entire school. This meant I was now one of a select few who had the great honor of singing at various school and community events.

After that first taste of schoolboy celebrity, it didn't take me long to discover that I enjoyed singing my ass off much more than falling on it. Clearly, this was a life lesson worth taking to heart—though over the years I'd eventually learn that singing my ass off and falling on it weren't mutually exclusive.

Just in case you haven't figured it out yet, the ugly truth is that I was never the ideal student—not even close. And once the mind-altering freedom and power of music hit me over the head, nothing else in life stood a snowball's chance in hell. Sports—which I've always loved, particularly basketball—could no longer compete. Girls—whom I desperately and increasingly *wanted* to love—generally weren't trying too hard to win my affection.

Last and assuredly least, there was that annoying matter of schoolwork, which I increasingly came to resent for carving such an outrageous chunk from my weekdays. With that kind of crappy attitude, it's not surprising I became a consistently mediocre student, and somewhere gathering dust in an Alabama storage facility are the crappy report cards to prove it.

The awful truth is that my academic career was fairly checkered even *before* I got into music. Music merely served to vanquish whatever earnest feelings I had about bearing down in school . . . *eventually.* What can I say? When it came to hunting down old R&B records that I really wanted—or even making a layup in basketball—I had tremendous interest and boundless energy. Yet somehow when it came time to actually hit the books, I became instantly tired, very tired.

I like to think that on some deep level I sensed that entertaining people was my calling—the thing I was *meant* to do. From that perspective, school was just a hindrance. Or so it seemed.

In my mind, focusing on schoolwork meant settling for a life far less interesting than the one I was secretly beginning to dream about—being a musical entertainer or even a star.

And so by the time I made my incredibly lazy way to senior year of high school, I'd pretty much opted out. Honestly, I don't believe I cracked a book that whole final year.

Thinking back over my boyhood, I can only remember one time when I dedicated real effort to getting good grades, and—gulp—that was the time I decided to make them up myself.

I perpetrated the scam during my sophomore year of high school. My dad was exerting pressure on me to turn things around and pick up my grades so I could get into a decent college. Back then, Dad wasn't pushing me toward any particular career, including his, but he made it very loud and clear—more loud than clear—that getting a college education wasn't optional.

Back then, I wouldn't have dared mention my dream of making music for a living—to my father or anyone else. I was smart enough to realize that a successful music career was an extreme long shot. So I just stayed quiet and nodded when my father said things like "Make something of your life" or "Don't be an idiot."

When it became obvious that I'd have to show some progress to appease him, I ruled out the daunting work involved in actually *earning* good grades and began searching for a shortcut. And thus it was that as I sat in the school cafeteria one afternoon, an especially dim lightbulb flickered on and off over my head.

That afternoon I stopped by the home of a friend whose

mother, conveniently, was in the burgeoning field of computerized design. Using some programs I found there, I began carefully, almost lovingly counterfeiting a report card. For perhaps the first time in my academic history, I was "in the zone." At long last, here was something vaguely to do with my schoolwork that left me feeling fully challenged and engaged. Reading, writing, and arithmetic had never quite done the trick for me, but in creating fake documents, I'd finally found myself something to which I could apply myself.

Unsurprisingly, my grade point average dramatically shot through the roof on my new report card—signaling nothing less than stunning improvement. If I was going to lie, I figured, why not go for the big lie? At last I could be—at least for one brief shining, self-deluded moment—that impressive A student my father had always wanted me to be. Ah, the thrill of it all.

Let me be the first to concede that faking a great report card is both shortsighted and thoroughly dishonest, but in the execution of my crime, I have to give myself high marks. Okay, my fraudulent report card may not have been a perfect imitation, with all the proper school markings. But I knew my parents' habits, and in my mind it was a dead certainty that when I handed them that card, they'd be focusing on one thing only: my grades.

It's with a mixture of pride and shame that I report that the scheme worked magnificently—at least until a few days later, when my math teacher, Mrs. Satterwhite, called my home to arrange a sit-down with my parents. The topic? My underwhelming academic performance.

Completely clueless that I'd awarded myself an A– in her class, Mrs. Satterwhite innocently phoned our place and informed my stepmother, "Taylor is having a problem with math." My stepmother was totally taken aback. "Well," she said a bit indignantly, "I could understand you feeling that way if Taylor hadn't earned an eighty-nine." At that point it was my teacher's turn to be taken aback. *"Eighty-nine?"* she said. "Taylor scored a *twenty-nine.* What report card are *you* looking at?"

With that the jig was up, and my punishment was swift. For the next month, the school decreed that I sit on the bench rather than play on the basketball team. And when I got home, I was pretty much benched there too—only for even longer. Looking back now on the whole episode, I think I got off pretty easy.

Just so you don't get the wrong idea, I want you to know that there were at least a few moments in school when I wasn't completely screwing up or trying my best to get myself hurt. Over the years, there were even a few teachers who were either deluded or forward-thinking enough to sense in me something worthwhile.

For example, when I was in ninth grade at Hoover High School, I had an amazing English teacher. Her name was

Susan Dryden, and I remember Miss Dryden always going out of her way to make a connection with me. Looking back, I think she made all of us in the classroom feel that way. Miss Dryden had blond hair and a big smile with a gleam in her eye—a really special sparkle. Something about her manner made me feel as if she understood me better than most people did back then.

One day after school Miss Dryden came up to me and very nicely handed me a book called *My Side of the Mountain* that she thought I might like to read. Truthfully, I was always more interested in reading the newspaper than throwing myself into a novel. But because of her personal recommendation, I decided to give it a shot. The story was about a kid who goes on a journey all by himself. I think my teacher was sensitive enough to understand that there was something hopeful in that story that would speak to my own sometimes lonely journey.

Down in my part of Alabama, we weren't much for talking to counselors and therapists about our problems—at least, not as far as I could tell. But by this time, I was getting a little more open about letting certain people know about what was going down on *my* side of the mountain. I think Miss Dryden understood just enough of the truth of my family situation to realize things weren't all that rosy.

With luck we've all had teachers who give a damn about the kids in their classroom. Well, Miss Dryden was undeniably one of those teachers. She was a dedicated teacher and an amazing lady who, I could have predicted, would go on to accomplish great things. Little did I know that she and I would meet again many years later under circumstances so remarkable that neither one of us could yet possibly imagine them.

Though my grades were typically shaky growing up, my social life tended to be on a solid footing. Even when things got tense at home, I always had friends—male and female. I was a fairly popular guy back in high school, though a bit of a wild child who was located somewhere between the jocks and the freaks. I suppose I was both a jock and a troublemaker. Put it this way: remember that odd kid who would sneak out and smoke cigarettes right after football practice? Well, that kid was me.

Mixing things up socially the way I did in high school would come in handy later, especially on *American Idol.* There, much like in high school, it's important at times to know how to be all things to all people.

By high school standards, I suppose I did okay with the ladies, though if you were to track down the girls nice enough to go out with me, they'd probably tell you I looked to them for some mothering as well. My romantic life actually began years earlier, and even today I wince a bit at my inauspicious start. Like me, the woman of my dreams was in fifth grade at the time.

Here's the story: summoning all of my courage, I asked a

girl at school by the name of Angie to go putt-putt golfing with me. Take it from someone who knows, performing on national TV and singing for millions is a lot easier than, at age ten, asking a girl you like to play some putt-putt with you. After giving the question due consideration, Angie eventually said yes, making me—for a day or so—the happiest fifth grader on earth.

Then at the appointed date and time, tragedy struck. For reasons I'll never know, Angie didn't show. I recall excitedly buying a bunch of red roses, then standing there holding them at the putt-putt course waiting in vain for Angie to appear. Those were some of the longest hours in my young life. In a way, I guess I'm *still* waiting for Angie—my dream girl who hasn't showed up yet.

After that fifth-grade heartbreak, I remember sitting in my room playing the song "Angie" by the Rolling Stones over and over again, perversely relishing the feeling of rubbing salt in a fresh wound. Not for the first or the last time, sad, soulful music helped me feel just a little better, somehow easing the pain of that awful putt-putt put-down.

Angie baby, wherever you are, I'd like to thank you right now, because the truth is that by standing me up that night, you probably saved me a lot of trouble and money over the years. I don't think I ever let my guard down that much again. That's the sad story of my very first date—not exactly a warm and fuzzy welcome to the wide world of romance, but one that left a lasting impression nonetheless.

As for another very big first in any young man's life, I'll confess here that I lost my virginity back when I was a highly excitable eighteen-year-old. I'd like to take this opportunity to thank that very special young lady for making that very pleasurable experience possible. For as long as the act lasted—which was not all that long, honestly—it was exceedingly welcome.

Thinking back on it, I don't remember ever getting much advice from my father about women. So here too, I made my own mistakes and learned most of my own lessons along the way.

After I won *American Idol,* history was rewritten to make me into some kind of American stud. Not only was I named "Hottest Bachelor" by *People* magazine, some of the more investigative entertainment reporters started digging into my romantic history. One dogged chronicler of our times even talked to my prom date, Taylor Brooke Kelly—yes, I dated a girl named Taylor too—who let the cat out the bag about my "navy plaid tux," conclusively proving I was not *always* the impeccable fashion plate I am today. She also remembered me as being a great dancer—something I'm rarely accused of.

The other Taylor also informed the reading world that I was "the center of attention" at the prom. Now, I don't remember prom night exactly that way, but I definitely received my fair share of attention back in school.

Inevitably, you learn a lot about getting attention—wanted and otherwise—when at fourteen your hair starts going gray.

By the time I was twenty, my hair was fully and forever frosty. The way I look at it now, life just made me grow up a bit earlier than most people, and I got the hair to go along with that reality.

Truthfully, things did get a little annoying early on when kids in class would try to pluck out a gray hair and have an easy laugh at my expense. When you're fourteen, you just want to fit in. But as I've already said, distinguishing characteristics can end up helping a person much more than they hurt.

So it's without any trace of bitterness that I hereby invite any of those kids who plucked out my gray hairs all those years ago to take a moment and go to the Taylor Hicks weblog, which is actually dedicated to me and my gray hair. It's called GrayCharles.com, and maybe we can have our next high school reunion there.

By the end of high school, I started to realize that the way I *really* wanted to get the world's attention was by singing and playing for people. Fortunately, there was a teacher at school named Mr. Chapman who was a good guitar player and had his own band. Mr. Chapman taught me a few blues chords that I've since gotten a lot of mileage out of. So at that point, in addition to singing and playing the harmonica, the guitar came into my life.

Before long, I was ready to take my chances in what would be my first talent show. It wasn't as high-profile as

American Idol, of course. It was held at Hoover High and the top prize was only a couple hundred dollars—with not even a major record deal thrown in. Still, I saw this as my big shot to become a star, at least within the walls of my high school. We all have to start somewhere.

Unfortunately, I was so excited about my looming public performance that I forgot to check the gas gauge when it came time to drive to the school. Soon enough, the gas pedal stopped responding. Fighting off panic, I ditched my car on the side of the road and began sprinting up the hill to Hoover.

Rushing into the auditorium just in time to take my turn onstage, I dared to perform my state's *real* national anthem, "Sweet Home Alabama" by Lynyrd Skynyrd. I sang as soulfully as I could and played some really bad harmonica. (That's *bad* as in good.) How was my stage presence? Well, let's just say that it matched my experience, which was none—unless you count the time my mom's dad volunteered me, at age six, to sing a little bit of a Hank Williams Jr. song at an old country barn in Clanton, Alabama. Still, something about my enthusiastic performance and shaky dancing was entertaining enough to help me take first place in the competition.

This win would prove to be a key stepping-stone in the long process of finding my voice and finding my way. It wasn't just that it was my first victory as an entertainer. It gave me a taste of something I realized I was hungry for—a sense of self-worth and the respect of my peers. From now on, I'd be working harder than ever to develop my skills. And if all that upside weren't enough, my triumph yielded yet another dividend—I was able to use a portion of my winnings to gas up my car.

That night I gleefully celebrated my first musical triumph with all my pals at Hoover High. I had no idea how many more lessons I still had left to learn.

5

IN MY TIME

TRIED TO FIND THE HEART

BUT IT WASN'T THERE

SO I TOOK THE HIGHWAY TO YOUR SOUL

ROLLING THUNDER SWINGING LOW

TAKE ME FURTHER ON DOWN THE LINE

HOPE TO FIND YOU IN YOUR TIME.

—"In Your Time" by Taylor Hicks

I t's a long and strange trip, going from squeezing out a tiny victory at a high school talent show in Hoover, Alabama, to winning big and becoming an actual American Idol. It's really not the kind of journey you can make all by yourself— at least *I* couldn't. So I consider myself blessed to have had a loving and supportive "family" that always seemed to be there looking out for me and pointing me forward in the right direction. The family I'm referring to wasn't my biological one, but it all worked out just fine.

In the very best way imaginable, the Black family— Richard and Susan Black and their two sons, Robert and Ryan—was a little unusual. So it's only right that I came to make their acquaintance under unusual circumstances. It was my sophomore year and I'd been dating a slightly older woman at school. Having just recently received my driver's license,

I decided I'd try to crash the graduating seniors' big beach party blowout in Florida—just to see what trouble I could get myself into there. I've never been a patient man, and frankly, the whole thing sounded like too much of a good time for me to have to wait until I was actually graduating—assuming I ever made it that far.

So I hit the road in my white Ford Probe, my very first car. Like my singing at the time, that car was very, very *white*. That wasn't going to stop me, though—I was bound for glory, or at least a good time. Well, when I got to Destin, Florida, on the Emerald Coast of the Florida Panhandle, it turned out the girl I'd been dating had also been dating another guy from my school—some dude I didn't really know named Robert Black. As you'd expect of someone who's dating two people at once, she was very slick, and perhaps sensing trouble from having us both in town, she just kind of disappeared from the weekend.

As chance would have it, though, I met up with my romantic nemesis, Robert, on the beach that same day. Instead of one of us kicking the other's ass, however, the two of us ended up standing there on the beach, our feet in sand, hitting it off just like we'd been buddies all of our lives. I think we both realized she probably wasn't worth the fight.

The two of us had come to Destin to cut loose and get crazy at the nastiest, dirtiest, and (in my now well-informed opinion) single greatest graduation party spot any irresponsible teenager could imagine. We were in the right place, all right. We were all staying at a motel called the Beach Mark.

Sadly, the Beach Mark is long gone now, so you can't go there and see it for yourself. To picture this place, just imagine the absolutely perfect run-down set for the film *Girls Gone Wild: The Gator Edition,* and you are *there.* This was exactly the kind of place where anything goes—and then some. Come to think of it, that may be the reason the place doesn't exist anymore. The Beach Mark was simply *too* good—or do I mean too *bad?*—to last, but it still left its mark on me.

That night, while we were all hanging out and partying at the Beach Mark, there was a guy with a guitar out on a balcony playing a little. In a rare moment of musical reticence, I'd left my harmonica in my car for the night. Thankfully, though, my brand-new best buddy, Robert, had already heard me play on the beach earlier that day, and he announced to anyone within earshot that they absolutely *had* to hear me. Tolerating no resistance, he ordered me to hurry up and get that harmonica out of my glove compartment and show the guests of the Beach Mark exactly what I could do.

Now, ever since I shocked my dad by playing along to Supertramp's "Take the Long Way Home," I'd been continuing to get better and better on the mouth harp just by fooling around with it during my free time. As I've said before, when it came to that instrument I was completely self-taught, but I was also sort of a natural. Every once in a while being a big blowhard comes in handy.

And because of my hard-won proficiency, that windy walk to my Ford Probe to fetch my harmonica ended being one of the most meaningful trips of my life. I owe a lot to Robert too. If he hadn't hyped me so hard, I never would have wound up sitting on the hotel balcony jamming away for hours as dozens of us looked out toward the surf and had the time of our lives.

Maybe it was Robert's advance rave review, or possibly it was just the way I was singing and playing, but suddenly I was the focus of a lot of attention, and I loved it. Before long, another party of people four or five floors away from us began watching, cheering, and clapping along to the sound the guitar player and I were making in all our ragged glory. It was a real kick—the kind of experience that makes you believe in your own magic.

Of course, to be fair, the fact that everybody in the vicinity of the Beach Mark was probably drunk out of their minds probably didn't hurt the reception we got.

Still, for me, it was the most beautiful sight imaginable: all these happy people hanging over their balconies watching me sing and play along with some wild tiki bar guitar player—and Robert Black cheering me on all the way, both of us totally forgetting that only hours earlier we'd met as romantic rivals.

That long breezy evening at the Beach Mark turned out to be more than just one great night. In my mind, that surfside jam session was my first big gig, even if the only payment was a few free drinks. I've had far larger gigs since, but that was still one hell of a live appearance.

More important, it was also the beginning of a beautiful friendship. When we returned home, Robert insisted I come over and meet his family. Always anxious for another place to be, I didn't take long to accept the invitation. I already knew I liked Robert and Ryan, Robert's younger brother, who was in my class at school. But I had no inkling yet that the Blacks' house would shortly become my new favorite—and more musical—home away from home.

When I first went to the Blacks', my initial and overriding impression was that there was music *everywhere.* Coming from a house where the air was, too frequently, filled with more tension than tunes, I felt like I was in a dream. I felt instantly at ease there.

The Blacks had their own music and their own endearing style. Susan Black—the sweetest lady in the whole world, as far as I can tell—so loved Elvis Presley that, simply by hanging out with her whenever I could, I learned to admire the man and his music more than I ever had before. As a devoted fan of the great black artists of R&B, I'd always resisted the King's call, but if Elvis was cool with Susan, he was okay by me.

Susan's husband, Richard Black, was a great guy in his own right and the first serious musician I'd met who took a real interest in me as a player. During the week Richard ran a very respectable business, but there was no doubt that at heart he was a musical weekend warrior. Whenever he accumulated a few extra dollars, instead of buying a lake house or joining some country club, he invested his money in musical instruments. He even formed a little club band that played the honky-tonks around lower Alabama—just for the love of it.

My overwhelming respect for the Black family became outright awe the first time I was ushered into their garage basement. To my stunned delight, they'd set up their very own ultra-cool sound room there—complete with PA system and, seemingly, every kind of musical instrument.

It was as if I'd died and gone to rock and roll heaven. For me, gaining entrance to that room was like being casually welcomed into Willy Wonka's chocolate factory or the Apollo Theater for a James Brown gig, only this was more convenient. Looking around the room that afternoon—with a few dazzling amplifiers set up right in front of me—I thought of begging the Blacks to adopt me.

Anyway, Robert and Ryan welcomed me into their club of brothers, and I became the third musketeer. Richard and Susan were like an extra set of parents—and good friends too. I quickly realized these were my people—close kin by choice.

Somehow things just kept getting better and better for me there. Back then, as I mentioned, Richard Black was in a band that would play on the weekends just for the hell of it. He played the keyboards. And sometimes he'd even let me sit in with his group and play while they practiced, giving me invaluable, hands-on experience. It was like a crazy dream— sort of the Partridge Family on Southern Comfort.

The Black family sound room turned out to be the ideal learning lab where I could experiment freely. In the days, months, and years to come, I'd spend many of my happiest and most formative hours there, fooling around with the instruments and discovering exactly how little I really did know.

The sound room boosted my happiness for an additional reason, though. Being a few years older and wiser than Ryan and me, Robert was the first to see that, rather than go out all the time to meet girls, it could be a lot more effective to invite women over, set up a mike or two, fire up an amp, and invite our guests to be part of the show. Right there in that confined space, I learned everything I ever really needed to know about music—and about life's *other* significant pleasures.

Most of all, what I loved about spending time at Chez Black was the presence of harmony. It's something I'd previously had little exposure to. Right from the start, the Blacks treated me as a member of the family—or at least a very special guest star.

One day I remember Susan taking a quick look at me when I walked in the door and commenting that I looked too skinny. With that, she scurried off to fix me up a giant plate of her special turnip greens. In the annals of fantastic maternal things women over the centuries have done for clueless teenagers, perhaps that gesture doesn't rank at the very top. But the reason the memory lingers after all these years is, well, the woman makes some *very* tasty turnip greens.

The Blacks lovingly treated me like I was one of their

own, and for that I'll never forget them. They haven't forgotten *me* either—not by a long shot. Traveling around as much as I do now, it's hard to keep track of every single thing written about me—not that I necessarily want to. Still, it moves me that Susan continues to keep a scrapbook of every Taylor Hicks mention she can find in newspapers and magazines.

The lessons the Blacks taught me helped make me the man and the musician I am. For example, Richard told me that if I wanted to be a true musician, I was going to have to learn to be an entertainer as well. "You can't just play to people," he'd tell me. "You have to *entertain* the crowd too." He made it clear that if you're going to sing, sing *out,* and sing it like you believe every word. And he let me know that as much fun as music could be, it was also something I'd have to take very seriously if it was going to add up to something.

Richard wasn't afraid to challenge me either. Susan recalls her husband sitting me down in the sound room one day and telling me if I was going to make it in the music business, I should learn how to really play guitar. Even more important, he told me that if I wanted to be a true musical artist, I had to try to write my own songs—not just blow harp to my favorite oldies. Knowing how much I liked to do things my own way, Susan wondered how I'd take to this strong direction.

Right after that lecture, I disappeared from the Black house for a couple of weeks, and Susan let it be known that she was worried about me. What was I doing? You guessed it: playing the guitar until my hands hurt. Also, sitting with a pen and paper and trying to write decent lyrics until my head hurt. When I finally returned to the Blacks, I could play guitar. And not long after, I sat everybody down in the sound room and played for them the very first song I ever wrote. It was called "In Your Time," and even if it did sound a bit too much like a certain Cat Stevens song I really loved, it was still pretty good for a rookie try. A few years later, "In Your Time" would become the title track of the first album I recorded on my own. So Richard's lecture paved the way for a number of firsts, the most important of which was that, for the *first* time in my life, I listened hard to somebody else and took their advice to heart.

Soon after I sang that debut song for them, Richard and Susan must have decided I was ready to take the plunge and discover what it's like to play for a potentially hostile crowd. So, throwing a big golf hat on me as a disguise—remember, I was under the legal drinking age—Richard drove us over to Corey's Sports Bar. Corey's was a slightly sketchy biker joint a little off the beaten track under the interstate in downtown Birmingham. That night a really good blues band was playing.

I was nervous—this sure wasn't my usual crowd—but even more excited as I jumped up on the tiny stage and tried my best to play some harp and keep up with the band, an interracial group with serious chops. Now, I may not have blown away the crowd with my playing. I *know* I didn't blow them away with my vocal take on "Stormy Monday"—but, thankfully, I lived to tell. Looking back, I think Richard recognized that the time had come to throw this blues baby in the pool to see if I'd sink or swim.

For everything they've done for me over the years without asking for anything in return, the Blacks will always have a special place in my career, and in my heart. I hereby confess there were a couple of times over the years when I daydreamed that the stork had dropped me onto the *Blacks'* doorstep instead of my slightly harder real-life landing. Ultimately, though, things worked out just fine for me in the end—because I eventually *did* wind up on their doorstep. I certainly arrived with more gray hair than most newborns, but the Blacks were kind enough to take me in anyway.

By the time my high school graduation day arrived, I was very much a young man who was ready to move on. The big question hanging in the air was where I'd be moving *to*. By this point, having really grown up in the Blacks' sound room, I was sure that all I wanted to do was make music. My father, on the other hand, was equally certain that what I needed to do was get a college education.

Now, I could look back on those days and say my dad was being unreasonable—but of course that wasn't the case. Truth be told, he was being entirely logical. Both musically and in so many other ways, I still had a lot to learn—and let's face it, my prospects for finding gainful employment in music weren't any more encouraging than those for any other wannabe with delusions of pop grandeur. Even in all my excitement about holding my own at Corey's and earning the Blacks' respect, I knew I was, by any fair standard, a total long shot.

And so, going against type for once, I tried—however halfheartedly—to do the right thing by my dad and myself. With no great commitment, I decided I'd go to college and—who knows—maybe even prepare myself for some sort of gainful employment while I was there.

By some fluke of good fortune, I was able to get into Auburn University in Auburn, Alabama—one of the largest universities in the South and, by most measures, an excellent institution. Auburn is an extremely pretty school on the scenic plains of eastern Alabama. I'd recommend it heartily to anyone who's serious about learning. I just wish that, when I was there, I'd been one of those people.

If you were to check my official record at Auburn— and please *don't*—you'd see that I studied journalism for a short time there: good preparation for all the media interviews I'd do later in my life. After that, I studied psychology but realized I had too many psychological problems of my own to help with other people's issues. Next I studied business and marketing, which would definitely come in handy for a guy who was going to have to struggle to make his name in music.

From my admittedly skewed and hazy perspective, more than half of what you learn in college has nothing remotely to do with what you learn in the classroom. In my case, it was even more than half—like 99 percent.

Whatever my official Auburn transcript says, don't believe any of it for a second. That's because, just between us, my *actual* undergraduate major was, in fact, barhopping—not so much to drink, mind you, as to play at great local venues like the War Eagle Supper Club on South College Street, where I was starting to find a steady gig. Inside the walls of the War Eagle I was a headliner. In the classroom, I didn't even qualify as an opening act. Guess which one I preferred.

In the end, despite my own worst efforts, college life *did* expose me to things and people that had a big impact. For example, being around a more eclectic crowd, my musical and social world expanded in new and interesting directions.

For a little while, technically matriculating if not actually *studying* at Auburn, I found myself performing with a pretty decent six-piece jam band called Passing Through, which played a lot of covers by popular groups like Widespread Panic, Phish, and others—including some that borrowed choice pages from the Grateful Dead's playbook.

How the relationship with Passing Through got started was that my buddy Chris Poole took me to a Sigma Chi fraternity house where the band was playing. I was only a freshman, and the band members were a cool bunch of juniors living in this big place called the Marquee at Auburn. The guys later told me that I arrived at their doorstep looking more like a timid schoolboy carrying a lunch box than a front-man prospect. Sizing me up as a freshman dweeb, they almost sent me away, but since I was already there they generously decided that they'd take a few minutes and give me a fair hearing.

They asked if I knew "The Thrill Is Gone" by B. B. King, which, being a man of some taste, I most surely did. The band performed the first verse without me, and then I jumped in with both feet. When I looked to my side, I noticed the guitar player, Mike Douglas, just staring at me with his mouth wide open. As soon as the song was done, he called me over and explained that they had a little gig in town the next night. Was there any way I could study up on some lyrics and sit in for their set? All of a sudden being a dweebish freshman didn't seem like such a big problem. Much later, Mike explained to me that when I opened my mouth to sing, he saw dollar signs before his eyes. His second thought was that I sure didn't sing like a white guy, which I took as supreme praise.

Helped by booze-fueled brashness, I began Passing Through's first set the next night with a version of the great Bill Withers' "Ain't No Sunshine." By the time I finished the last song of the night, I believe I was officially in the band.

Musically speaking, I was more a soul singer than a Deadhead, so I let the other guys sing a lot of stuff that didn't suit me well. On those numbers, I'd just blow a little harmonica or tap a little tambourine. Of course, it didn't require a lot of encouragement for me to go front and center to belt out

Wilson Pickett's "Mustang Sally" or "Whipping Post" by the Allman Brothers.

We ended up pulling a real band together and signing with a little agency in Nashville that was able to book us in all sorts of clubs, juke joints, and frat parties across the Southeast. One night we'd play to hundreds of kids at a cool club in Oxford, Mississippi; the next we'd be at some dump in Jacksonville, Alabama, that had tree stumps as bar seats for like five people. Once I got past all that eye-straining tie-dye, I felt pretty much at home in the whole hippie-trippy, free-form jam band scene.

Why? Because, for most jam bands—and for me as well—the thrill of making music is putting everything you've got into your live performance. When you're onstage, that's when you're most alive as a musician. As much fun as it can be to play music by yourself, there's no replacement for that live-wire energy and indefinable interplay between you and your audience. Yes, recordings are important, but for me, the show's the thing.

Playing in Passing Through, I met someone who to this day continues to play a major role in my life—someone I still talk to daily. Back then, Mike Douglas was my guitar player. These days he's my lawyer, and a damn fine one at that. He's a man I'd trust with my life—and since he's my lawyer, I may very well have to sometime. As a guitarist, Mike is pretty good, but as a lawyer, the guy riffs like Eddie Van Halen—

though I'm pretty sure Mike still bills me at a lower rate than Eddie would.

We had a lot of good times in Passing Through, including our very first brush with a big-time touring act. One summer break we were playing a couple of gigs at the beach stage of Flora-Bama, a club in the Gulf Shores area of Alabama. The place was one big, rowdy beach party where you'd have so much fun you'd happily play just for a bar tab. Some New York agent type who was way out of place there came up to us during a break and told us that the country singer Doug Supernaw—known for songs like "I Don't Call Him Daddy," "Reno," and "Daddy Made the Dollars (Mamma Made the Sense)"—wanted to come up to play with us.

Within seconds, this actual big-time country star had jumped up onstage in cutoff shorts and a wife-beater shirt and said, "What do you boys want to play? Do you know 'Sweet Home Alabama'?" Now, we didn't play it, but of course we *knew* it—especially me, considering it had been my very own winning number at the high school talent show. The crowd went suitably insane—the single loudest reaction Passing Through ever received.

Afterward, Supernaw invited our band to come have a beer in his giant, gorgeous tour bus. It was bigger than our homes, and nicer too. He then insisted that he wanted to see how we traveled, so we introduced him to the full glory of our little old Chevy conversion van. He stretched out on the tiny back bench and said, "You know what—this is nice." We said, "No, this is a piece of shit. Your tour bus, *that's* nice."

Passing Through never made it to the big-bus stage. The band's time was running out, especially since the other guys were graduating and Mike was going off to law school to pursue a slightly more honest living. In May 1998, we played our last show at the Supper Club to a crowd of something like a thousand people. It was enough like The Band's famous *Last Waltz* concert that later we wondered why the hell we were breaking up.

Auburn was full of good bands then—including Spoonful James and one of my favorites, Iratowns, which was named after a local preacher who let the guys practice in his church. After my Passing Through phase, I put together a strange sort of Auburn all-star band called Fletch Lives—and no, we weren't as good as the movie. We chose the name because, just like Chevy Chase in *Fletch Lives,* the band had a whole different character every time. Is it any wonder Fletch Lives never made it big?

In the end, leaving Passing Through behind and creating my own band was about exerting control. When I got together with guys to play, I wanted to express *my* musical sensibility, even if that meant not fitting into any particular musical genre. Rightly or wrongly, I'd probably gotten too big for my britches for jam band membership anyway.

Not that I wouldn't have a few more brushes with jam band culture. Years later, I even got myself booked as a low-level solo act on one of those big Jam Cruises—basically a giant party boat where the entertainment consists not of Vegas lounge lizards but neo-hippie bands. At first, the cruise was one big tie-dyed blast. I was one of the smaller acts onboard, but my little acoustic gig went down pretty well. In fact, Les Claypool—an amazing musician most famous for playing with Primus—was there and he generously took the time to compliment me on my performance. That small gesture really made my day.

Unfortunately, my day was soon unmade. Apparently, my gray head of hair and relatively conservative manner of dress started to rub some of the jam-loving voyagers the wrong way. Even on this giant ship of gleefully freaky folks, I somehow didn't quite fit in. A couple of especially paranoid stoners got it into their confused dead heads that I was *not* an obscure, struggling working musician but an undercover narc from the FBI sent on the seven seas to kill their buzz.

To my utter amazement, the crazy rumor spread that I was the Man riding the waves just to bust up the party. Hell, it wasn't exactly like I was wearing a dark three-piece suit on the sun deck. I had on a collared shirt, jeans, and a nice pair of tennis shoes. For a few tense hours there, I kind of wished I *did* have a badge. Unfortunately, as anybody who actually knows me understands full well, I was in absolutely *no* position to bust anybody else.

♫

When I left Passing Through, I decided the time had come for me to do my own thing—hey, who better to play Taylor Hicks music? Full of confidence from becoming a semicelebrity on campus—and possibly full of myself—I didn't want to wait around anymore for some record company to discover me. And so I decided to make a record on my own dime—of which I still had very, *very* few.

Here's the thing you young musicians out there must understand before ever trying something like that: when you're paying to produce your own album, the clock is *always* ticking, so whatever happens—and something *always* happens—you're the one writing the check for every tick that tocks. My first recording, *In Your Time,* had seven tracks—a mix of my original songs ("Son of a Carpenter," "The Fall," "Somehow," and the title track) and my cover versions of "On Broadway," originally made famous by the Drifters; "Tighten Up," first funkified by Archie Bell and the Drells; and finally, "Georgia on My Mind," written by Hoagy Carmichael and Stuart Gorrell but forever owned by the real Man himself, Ray Charles.

To cut costs, I recorded the songs live, with only the slightest notion of what the hell I was doing. In the end the album cost me something like $4,500—a relatively low price that I was able to handle only with the generous help of my father and grandmother. Secretly, I assumed that the *In Your Time* album would be a smash and that major labels would trip over themselves rushing to Alabama to sign me to a lifetime deal.

I assumed wrong.

In the end, I pressed up something like fifteen hundred copies of *In Your Time* and sold only a fraction. I went to the DJs in Auburn and tried to get them to play it. I sent it to all the record companies, or at least I *tried* to in my low-budget way. I should have sent them first-class, but I mailed them all the cheapest, slowest way, and I'm not sure they ever even got to the people I intended.

As far as I know, I only got one little taste of airplay—and that was from Wildman Steve at Tiger 95.9. Today, that album is highly sought after; back then, I could scarcely give it away. If you're really, really desperate to see a photo of me with a mangy beard and mustache, by all means try to track down a copy.

Even after getting my first big hint that breaking into the music industry wouldn't be simple, I decided during senior year that I could no longer in good faith deny the waiting world my singular talent, not for a minute or—more to the point— a semester longer. Even if recording a CD myself hadn't made me rich—and clearly, it hadn't—I felt as if I'd learned a thing or two from doing it. Something about the experience of putting myself out there like that only made me hungry for more—much more. And "more," in my mind, meant that the time had come for me to leave my college days behind.

In the end, I'm embarrassed to confess that I dropped out of Auburn University with only thirty credits left to go before graduation—effectively wasting a whole lot of my father's money and a lot of my own time. One of the *good* things the Hicks family taught me was the value of work, and I was ready to go to work on my music *right then.* So instead of doing the appropriate thing and completing my academic career, I decided in the throes of my musical passion to cut my losses and hit the bars so that I could stake my claim to fame.

In my heart, I knew that the sort of education I yearned for now was the kind you could only get in bars and roadhouses, not in classrooms. Like Kanye West, I became a college dropout, but rest assured that I'd never name an album after that achievement—or lack thereof. There'd be times when I regretted my impatience and my insensitivity to my family's wishes. Upon leaving school, I didn't have to ask my father if I'd made him proud—like in that song I'd someday be asked to sing—because I knew I hadn't.

What can I say? College is a great thing for most people, but as you've probably figured out by now, I'm not most people. For a million probably lousy reasons, I just couldn't take even another moment to do the right thing. As I saw it, the time had finally come to try to do the only thing I ever wanted to do.

6

LOST AND FOUND
IN MUSIC CITY

LOOK AT THE PEOPLE AROUND YOU
STABBING AT YOUR HEART
BUT YOU STILL SMILE IN KINDNESS
FOR NOT KNOWING WHO THEY ARE

AND THEIR STORIES HAVE ENDED
AND THEY'VE LIT UP THE TOWN
AND IT'S TIME TO GO HOME
AS THEY LIE THEIR BODIES BACK DOWN

THERE'S TOO MANY THINGS LEFT TO BE UNSAID
SO I LIVE IN A DARK HOLE
SOMETIMES IN MY HEAD

BUT I'M ALL RIGHT
I'LL GET BY
SOMEHOW.

—"Somehow" by Taylor Hicks

School was out now and the twenty-first century was in. It was the winter of 2000, and at long last I was 100 percent free to follow my music wherever it would take me. Perversely, as it would turn out, my muse and Interstate 65 northbound were now taking me and my 1994 Ford Explorer Sport on a frigid winter afternoon from Birmingham, Alabama, to one of the legendary capitals of great American music—Nashville, Tennessee.

Having impulsively tossed away the safety of Auburn University, I was now committing the dangerous act of putting everything I had right on the line. Of course, it didn't *seem* that dangerous at the time. In fact, it seemed downright sensible. Given my career aspirations, moving to the place they call Music City USA seemed like the most professional thing I could do.

Even as I was getting ready to leave Birmingham and saying farewell to my friends and family there, I knew I'd never forget my sweet home Alabama. However, I didn't have too much time for sentiment. I was now a man on a quest—a man determined to establish myself on a national level. Like Woody Guthrie and so many others before me, I was bound for glory—or so I thought.

For a couple of years now, I'd been playing regular gigs back home in Alabama and getting, I felt, progressively better. Backed by the first of what would be countless editions of the Taylor Hicks Band, I sang cover versions of the songs I loved, and even a few originals I'd somehow cobbled together out of my various musical influences. But with every new season that passed without my turning into a superstar, I couldn't shake the awful, nagging feeling that I was running on a hamster wheel—couldn't help picturing myself as a comic figure going nowhere at a very rapid pace.

I loved Birmingham—then *and* now—but at that precise moment my musical ambition was playing catch-up with my musical passion. No longer, I vowed, would anyone mistake my music for some hobby or passing fancy. When you want something badly, you want the world to take your dream as seriously as you do. So now I didn't just work at *making* music—I worked at making it *in* music. I was suddenly and overwhelmingly desperate to get somewhere.

By any measure, Nashville was not just somewhere. My goal was clear: to get a major-label record deal. And it seemed a whole lot more likely I'd find one in Nashville, Tennessee, where the major labels actually did business on a daily basis, than in my own backyard. Such was the arrogance of my fleeting youth that I figured if others could do it, I could too. If Ray Charles could have a run of country hits, as he famously did starting in the early sixties with songs like "I Can't Stop Loving You," "Crying Time," and "Born to Lose," then maybe Taylor Hicks could scare up a couple of chartbusters while he was there too. And so nearly forty years after Brother Ray made history with his classic crossover album *Modern Sounds in Country and Western Music,* I found myself excitedly if nervously loading up my beat-up little truck with the bulk of my earthly possessions—including a large box of unsold *In Your Time* albums—for the three-hour drive from my hometown to the home of the Opry, the capital of country music, the place where I'd take my rightful place as a star.

Thinking back on it now, I can conjure up the excited, hopeful feeling I had driving into Nashville on that very first snowy evening. The entire Music City appeared before me like one big clean slate. For one night at least, Nashville looked exactly like I'd hoped it would be—a place of truly limitless promise where I'd undoubtedly make my mark.

And then the next morning I woke up.

You might think that at some point on my long ride to Nashville—which included, I'll now confess, a Waffle House pit stop—it would have dawned on me that my new plan for world domination had one small hitch. Okay, one *huge* hitch.

But, truthfully, I never paused long enough to consider what should have been glaringly obvious: whatever else I might have been, I was—for better or worse—no country singer.

Sure, my idol Ray Charles had successfully made the leap between musical genres with amazing grace, but he was the one and only Brother Ray, the Genius of Soul. Tragically, I was no genius. Rather, I was one of the world's youngest, palest, and most obscure old-school soul singers. When I spoke, I might *sound* country, but when I sang, I was, for better or worse, just a soul man. To think otherwise was really just a case of pure foolishness and racial profiling.

Like a million other American hopefuls over the past half century, I'd come to Nashville with the dream of becoming a star. I was there to be discovered, appreciated, well paid, and consumed. It was simply how people did things before the gods invented *American Idol.* And for the most part, it remains the way the game is still played in country music today.

So I moved into a tiny apartment off West End Avenue, not far from the popular clubs on Lower Broadway where many of the greats had gotten their breaks. The place would set me back $350 a month, but I figured that wasn't too big a nut to cover now that I'd started my countdown to wealth and fame.

Having gotten a small but delicious taste of acceptance in the clubs around Auburn, I fully expected to blow Nashville away with my unique and radiant talent. Within days, I figured, I'd take my rightful place not simply at the top of the charts but in the musical pantheon.

I figured wrong. Instead, what happened was . . . well, nothing happened. *Nothing.*

In a town so full of music, the silence that greeted my arrival was deafening. Like every other starry-eyed singing hopeful, I made the rounds, looking for that first true believer in my talent. Result? I spent a full *year* knocking on the doors of Music Row—doors that would never really open up. I hustled tapes of my songs to anyone I could pawn one off on. But even giving my music away that way, I couldn't stir up any real interest in me as a Nashville recording artist or songwriter.

Putting your heart and soul out there day after day to be judged by the powers that be can be horribly soul-crushing. And after getting consistently steamrolled, I began retreating further and further into my own head. For the better part of the next bleak year I stayed in my apartment writing song after song, hoping to finally compose one that would get me noticed. Sometimes I could smell that big break hiding just around the corner, but the truth is, I never even got close.

Occasionally I would luck into the opportunity to try to write with one of the town's countless fine songwriters— a welcome break in the monotony that didn't make me any actual money but at least broke up my increasing sense of frustration and isolation. It wasn't enough, though. My stay in Nashville was turning into one of the loneliest, most depressing times of my entire life. I didn't really know anyone there, and despite the town's southern cordiality, none of the residents seemed in a particular rush to get to know me either.

For no shortage of reasons, I soon discovered that the country music industry, based downtown on Music Row, didn't know what the hell to do with someone like me—and didn't much care.

In all fairness to the good people of Nashville, this over-whelming lack of interest shouldn't really have come as too big a surprise, especially since I wasn't exactly your typical hunky country music kind of guy. When it came to signing male singers, everybody on Music Row was busy looking for the next Tim McGraw. Unfortunately, even then I looked more like Dr. Phil McGraw than the man who gets Faith Hill on a regular basis.

Truth be told, there were probably countless excellent reasons to say no to me back then. Whether or not you happen to think I can sing my ass off, a seriously depressed, slightly overweight, gray-haired R&B bar singer was just *not* going to cut it with the major labels in the country music capital. When, these days, I look at some puffy pictures of me from that period—and given the choice, I'd much prefer to look the other way—I think even *I* might have passed on me, and I'm my biggest fan. I may have been just twenty-three years old back then, but I looked more like I was fifty and heading nowhere fast. The fact is, in moving to Nashville I hadn't really gone anywhere—I'd just traded one hamster wheel for another, only this one didn't pay as well.

My new life in Music City was made all the more miserable by the painful fact that I couldn't score a paying gig in Nashville to save my life. Not only couldn't I get signed, I couldn't even get booked. I think it all came down to the amount of competition in the immediate area. Each day in Nashville a whole new army of dreamers marched into town and, for the chance to be heard, lined up at the clubs to perform free of charge in front of an open mic. More than anywhere else on earth, the local music market was wildly and continuously oversaturated. If anywhere near Nashville you wanted to get a good gig that paid—well, bless your heart if you weren't Tim McGraw.

Emotionally and financially, I am a man who lives to play live, but back then the only steady gigs I could score were in the clubs back home in Alabama. And so, just a matter of weeks after I first arrived in Nashville on that snowy night, I found myself reversing course. Each weekend I drove three hours so that I could scare up a few much-needed dollars in Birmingham. That way I could almost—and I stress *almost*—afford to keep hitting my head against walls in Nashville during the week.

One time, I remember driving back to Nashville through the night after a little homecoming gig in Birmingham. This time, when I got to the edge of town at three in the morning, there was no perfect white blanket of fresh snow, no sense of limitless possibility. My clean slate in Music City was already sullied, and now there was a whole different kind of chill in the air. I didn't know what I was doing there anymore. Still, I drove to my apartment and tried to get some rest, but I couldn't sleep at all.

For no good reason, I got dressed again at four in the morning and went for a walk on Lower Broadway, where all the clubs, stores, and bars had long since shut down for the night. Even with most of the neon lights turned off now, something about the place drew me in. I made my way past some of the cool clubs that I could never get myself booked into—like Tootsie's Orchid Lounge, where great singer-songwriters like Willie Nelson and Kris Kristofferson had taken their outlaw stands and somehow lived to tell. I walked past Robert's Western World and the Ernest Tubb Record Shop, first opened in 1947 by Tubb himself—one of the founding fathers of honky-tonk music who brought the world gems like "I'm Walking the Floor over You," "Tomorrow Never Comes," and "I'll Get Along Somehow." Ernest was long gone now, but you could still find his albums in the store. I wondered what the chances were that *I'd* ever have an album in the racks. More and more, I liked my odds in town less and less.

Finally, I turned off Broadway and walked up the hill to the historic and still exquisite Ryman Auditorium, the mother church of country music and the longtime site of the Grand

Ole Opry a few blocks away, and then for a long time I walked in circles around the place.

Now, I was no country music scholar any more than I was a country singer, but I still knew what this majestic place meant to music. Everyone from Roy Acuff to James Brown to Elvis Costello played the Ryman, bringing countless music lovers like me into its pews. But my favorite Ryman story was the one about how Johnny Cash himself once kicked out the stage lights in anger and then fell out of favor in Nashville for a time. In that moment of exhaustion and depression, I somehow felt very close to the Man in Black. I too was trying to walk a line now. And even without having kicked anything in particular, I—like Johnny before me—had fallen out of favor. At least, that's how it felt. In truth, my situation was far worse—I'd never been *in* favor.

Things got so depressing for me during those increasingly long weeks in Nashville that often the highlight of my day was going to Vandyland—a great down-home sweets and sandwich spot near the Vanderbilt University campus, where I'd eat and drink my sorrows away, in the process getting even heavier and less likely to fit into the scene.

After that, I'd go back to my little apartment with its lovely view of the Outback Steakhouse. The only real entertainment I had was the strange woman upstairs, whom I'd constantly hear loudly sandpapering her walls every night for hours on end. It was a horrible sound—almost as if her negative mental energy were shooting right through me. For the life of me, I could never figure out exactly what was going on with that lady, but I imagine she's rubbed herself right through those walls by now. I didn't know what she was doing up there, but then again I didn't know what I was doing either. In retrospect, it strikes me that she and I had more in common than I ever would have cared to admit.

But rather than go the sandpaper route, I decided I should spend every night—and day—writing songs. If I'd had more friends in town, I might have been out with them in bars *talking* about writing songs. But with no gigs and nothing but time on my hands, I mostly just stayed home and wrote until my hands hurt.

In my overwhelming frustration with life in Nashville and my place in the food chain, songs suddenly started pouring out of me. They were songs about heartbreak, songs about misery, songs that felt as though they were coming from my heart and soul.

I wrote songs about every girl who'd ever broken my heart, and every girl whose heart I'd broken. I wrote about girls I *wish* had broken my heart. After eventually running out of girls' names to use, I wrote songs about all my frustrations and fears—which, by the way, were growing by leaps and bounds. I had fewer and fewer prospects, but more and more material.

Not all the songs I wrote were great. Hell, not all of them were decent. But with every song I learned something about writing, and every once in a while I even learned something about myself.

And so despite all the negativity, and despite all the rejection, my sometimes hellish Nashville period ended up becoming a big positive. More than anything, Nashville is about writing a song that touches people or excites them. I was losing hope that anyone in town would ever sign me or even notice I existed. But as I lost hope and became every bit as depressed as the people in a lot of your finer country songs, I found I was starting to write the best songs I'd ever written—not for country radio, but for me, a soul singer caught in the wrong place at the wrong time.

Willie Nelson—who sang one of my favorite duets of all time, "Seven Spanish Angels" with Ray Charles—once said that we create our own unhappiness and that the purpose of suffering is to help us understand that we are the ones who cause it. Willie always struck me as one happy man, so I took his words to heart. A big lesson that got reaffirmed for me in Nashville is that if you're unhappy, you shouldn't just sit around wallowing in misery—rather, go out and do something to change your life. If *you* don't change it, who else will?

In my case, I came to realize that the validation I sought—and the remuneration I needed—simply *wasn't* going to be found in Music City, at least not by me. Unlike Carrie Underwood, I didn't appear destined to be a big country music idol. In looking for a new home base, I'd made my first big mistake, a misstep that had taken me a couple hundred miles in the wrong direction. To quote a good old country tune I probably couldn't sing, I'd been looking for love in all the wrong places, and it was time to stop and look elsewhere.

I'm a great believer in fighting your hardest to make your dream come true, but that doesn't exempt you from picking your battleground wisely. So far, I'd shown the battleground-picking savvy of George Armstrong Custer.

I remember one of the few times I got the chance to talk to someone at a record company with the power to sign me. The man from the A&R department of Sony Nashville looked me straight in the eye and handed me back my tape. "Listen, son, you're *not* going to make it in this town," he told me plainly but politely. "If you're ever going to get your deal, you're going to get it in Los Angeles. Good luck."

Realizing I wasn't going to take Music City by storm, I started dreaming of an alternative path. I decided I'd drive around the South playing anywhere I could actually get paid to play. If I couldn't make it here in Nashville, I figured, maybe I could still make it somewhere else. I'd move back to Birmingham as soon as possible, not to stay, but just to drop off my stuff, put my band back together, and scare up as many gigs as I possibly could.

Feeling trapped inside my own failure in Nashville, I thought I should now make the road my home—just as so many other dedicated music men had done before me. I'd no longer be a resident of Music City, but a true troubadour.

So with no regrets, and only some good songs to show for my time there, I got back in my car and left Nashville for life as a full-time road warrior.

Heading back home on the interstate, passing the Waffle House that had been a pit stop in so many trips back and forth, it struck me that if I was going to make it, I was going to have to do it not by fitting in but by standing out.

The call came on my cell phone just days after I arrived in Birmingham. It was the booker from 3rd & Lindsley—one of the hippest clubs in all of Nashville. Not realizing he was now talking to someone who was already a world away emotionally and three hours away geographically, the guy asked if I could hurry over to the club and play a show that evening. It was, of course, *exactly* the kind of call I'd been waiting for my entire time there.

For one of the only times in my life, I told the man I couldn't make the gig that night. At long last—and just when it didn't matter anymore—I finally had my small moment of vindication from Music City. It felt good to be asked to play, but I'd already moved on, and there was no looking back now.

7
HIT THE ROAD JACK

WHERE THE CITY STREET MEETS THE COUNTY ROAD,

WHERE THE SUN IS NICE AND WARM,

NO MATTER HOW LONG I MAY ROAM,

THIS SONG STILL TAKES US HOME,

TAKES US HOME.

—"Soul Thing" by Taylor Hicks

In my dreams, I envisioned returning to Birmingham from Nashville as music's latest rising sensation. Upon my arrival, I'd instantly become the center of attention at a steady procession of homecoming parades, limo rides down Main Street, and sold-out concerts. My grand tribute would culminate with the mayor of Birmingham declaring the day Taylor Hicks Day and officially presenting me with the key to the city as TV cameras lovingly documented my each and every move.

Naturally, all eyes would be on me the entire time, and all ears would bend to hear each and every note that I generously deigned to sing for all the good folks back home who'd made everything possible for me. Everyone in town—from little kids to sweet old grandparents—would cheer resoundingly when I walked by and gaze upon me almost as if I were some kind of, well, *idol.*

At least, that's the way things were *supposed* to happen. Sadly, as I unpacked my meager worldly goods into my empty new apartment on Birmingham's South Side and scrounged for some hand-me-down furniture with which to fill it, there was no denying that my fantasy of becoming a homecoming hero hadn't come to pass—at least not *yet.*

Against all odds and any sort of logic, I actually *would* get to live out my fantasy—or something eerily like it—later down the line. But such a warm reception remained a long, *long* way off. Thanks to *American Idol,* I'd get there eventually, but only by way of the most indirect and bumpy route imaginable.

Anyone expecting Taylor Hicks to return to Birmingham from Nashville as a broken man with a cowboy hat in hand would have been sorely disappointed. I've never been one to remain flat on the canvas for long, so I returned with my head still held high, a little bloodied but unbowed, ready to get right down to work.

In an odd way, failure had only made my ambition grow. This time I was going to try to conquer not just the country music industry but something far bigger—the whole damn country. Instead of simply picking out another new town— like New York or Los Angeles—to try my luck, I'd bring my music directly to any city that would have me.

Of course, I needed the right band—one that could back me all the way. And not just *a* band this time but *my* band. Consistent with that goal, rather than try to come up with another cute band name like Passing Through or Fletch Lives, I decided that my next group would be called one thing only—the Taylor Hicks Band. Something about those words had a ring to it, and there could be no confusion about who was ultimately in charge.

Win, lose, or draw, I was going to have to do things *my* way from now on, and really, I could leave no room for losing or drawing. The Taylor Hicks Band would have to be the sort of consistently winning live act that couldn't be denied. This time I would be searching not for a band of brothers or a band of equals but rather for a band that was capable of taking me wherever I needed to go.

Putting that kind of group together wouldn't be easy— particularly on my budget. When it comes to finding the perfect backing band, there are two qualities one must look for. The first—as you might imagine—is technical skill. But as Richard Black had often told me, there are a lot of good technicians out there. Being able to play the notes is only part of the gig. The second quality is an understanding of what it is to be part of a musical unit—the need to come *together* onstage to entertain people.

Even without holding auditions, I was confident I could find guys like that, or at least develop them. Still, when I waded into the task, I realized it was a whole lot more challenging than how they made it look on the sitcom *The Partridge Family*. Often I reflected on how truly fortunate Shirley Partridge had been to have all that cheap in-house talent—not to mention a cool Technicolor school bus.

Actually, as it turned out, the most complex part of my new job as a bandleader would not be finding the right people but holding on to them—especially since there wouldn't be much money to pay them.

Over the ensuing years, there were so many members of the Taylor Hicks Band that there were times when even I couldn't keep them all straight. If Spinal Tap had a pesky problem with exploding drummers, then the Taylor Hicks Band suffered especially from rotating bass players. Thankfully, some people stuck. I had a guitar player who was a little older than me named John Cook who must have stayed for eight years. He was both a great guitarist and a great guy.

Patrick Lunceford, a former drummer with our jam band Passing Through, would keep the beat and keep the faith for many years too—though during many of them the two of us would bicker like an old married couple.

Keeping a working band like ours together often came down to one unavoidable reality—to eat all the time, you had to play all the time. Being in Nashville had helped turn me into a songwriter. Now, being a bandleader helped make me a man, a professional, and an entertainer—three things I was desperate to be.

I learned countless lessons from leading a band—some much harder than others. For example, I learned all about hiring and firing. Here's what I finally figured out: whether you're running a band or running a hardware store, most of the same rules apply. An important rule is that you have to hire good people who make you look even better. This turns out to be especially true with a band because the skills are so specialized.

A band is also a lot like a sports team—something I'd had a little experience with back in high school. Like a coach, a bandleader constantly struggles to find the most winning combination he can put on the field. And also like a coach, a bandleader needs backups because sooner or later—usually when it's least expected—somebody is going to quit or get hurt or get his girlfriend pregnant and jump off your active player list. When nobody in a band is getting rich, you just never know when someone's going to leave. Sometimes your best player will just step out of the van at a rest stop and exit your life. Still, you keep going to the next gig, and you have to give it your best because, well, that's all you can do.

Having written myself a new mission statement, I assembled the first edition of the Taylor Hicks Band and hit the clubs, roadhouses, and assorted dive bars of the American South. We hit the road all right, and damned if it didn't take long before the road started to hit back.

To the outside world, the life of a working musician can seem like a summer breeze, one big carefree lark, a constant all-night party offering players money for little or no work and all the romance and booze they can imagine. If only it were so.

Sure, there are times when the road can be absolutely everything it's cracked up to be—and even a little bit more. And, yes, when you're living your life entertaining people in bars, you're going to spend a lot of time in close proximity to free drinks and relatively cheap women. (I'm talking from the *male* musician's point of view, of course.) But take it from somebody who's been there, making your living— and home—on the road *isn't* the path of least resistance.

Today, I'm blessed to have all sorts of talented and smart people on my team—managers, lawyers, agents, and accountants. Now that I'm a certified *American Idol,* somehow it takes a village to raise a Taylor Hicks. Yet during my road-band phase I was virtually all on my own, playing many parts and largely making it up as I went along.

One of the things I had to learn how to do was act. Back in my school days, I'd played the Easter Bunny twice, but a higher level of thespian accomplishment was required to secure gigs all over the East Coast and beyond. In the beginning I'd just look up the number of a club and try to cold-call my way into a brand-new gig. Sitting in my trashed-out bachelor pad, I'd put on my most professional music-industry voice and start pitching. My end of the conversation would go something like this: "Good afternoon, I'm calling you today about a really great young group down here in Birmingham. They're called the Taylor Hicks Band . . . That's H-I-C-K-S. These guys are *really* heating up all over the place now. You might know some of the boys from their old bands, Passing Through or maybe Fletch Lives. . . . You haven't, huh? Well, the lead singer, he's a helluva front man, and the guy plays some mean harmonica too. The whole band is packed with kick-ass players. You've got to hear 'em to believe them. . . . Their sound? I'd have to say that they're a little bit of everything you've ever loved and a whole lot of fun to watch. . . . What kind of material do they do? They do all sorts of great old-school soul covers and some rocking originals too. Heck, for the right price they'll probably do your laundry as well. And since we're talking price now, why don't we do some business right now? . . . What's *my* name? Sir, my name is Taylor Hicks, H-I-C-K-S."

My pitches weren't always well received, but every once in a while my gumption and persistence paid off. Believe it or not, my musical used-car salesman act actually worked quite often. Okay, I might not get us booked on a Friday or Saturday night, but more often than you'd think the club manager would slip us in on a quiet Monday or Tuesday just to get me off the phone.

Perhaps my business studies at Auburn really *had* paid off after all.

Even at our low, low discount prices, there were plenty

of nights when the Taylor Hicks Band got stiffed or short-changed. That's simply the nature of a tough business. And since I was now the bandleader—as well as road manager, roadie, and chief driver—that meant there were many nights when I got screwed and the guys in the band got paid out of my pocket. Unfortunately, that sort of thing just seems to come with the territory.

Down on the lower end of the music business food chain, where the Taylor Hicks Band was trying its damndest to squeeze out a living, we got used to being ripped off a little. It was expected—a well-established show business tradition, you might say. It was the times when we got ripped off a *lot* that killed me, and sometimes I'd have to stand up for myself.

I'm a singer, not a fighter, but even I have my limits—and there were a few times with the band when push really did come to shove. I remember one particularly tense confrontation right around the time the band was formed. By some stroke of luck, I'd booked us to play in a saloon that must remain nameless on the weekend of the big Ole Miss–Arkansas football game in Oxford, Mississippi.

This was the kind of booking I dreamed of back then—and one that still sounds awfully good even now. See, when you're lucky enough to be a nationally known name act in music—you know, the kind with a record deal and legions of fans—the simple fact that you're coming to town and playing a concert becomes, in and of itself, a true event.

But if you're still building up your name and following—

and attempting to eke out a living while you're doing it—
you have to try to hitch your star to anything big going on
around you. If you're going to be in a band, by all means
jump on any bandwagon you can. Take it from my experience, it's a whole lot easier to draw a big crowd to your show
when there's already a big crowd milling around looking for
something to do.

Down South at least, the weekend of a big football game
is perfect for a struggling band. Before the game everybody's
looking for something to do and someplace to drink. Then
after the game is over, win or lose, there are tens of thousands of people leaving the stadium looking for somewhere to
drink, eat, and maybe even listen to a little music so they can
either celebrate or drown their sorrows. In the Taylor Hicks
Band, we *lived* for those big football weekends.

That weekend at Ole Miss was one of those rare times
when the plan seemed to play out perfectly. Probably five or
six hundred kids came walking through the door that evening, each of them paying a cover charge of $8 apiece. We
were playing strictly for the door—that cover charge—while
the club made all its money at the bar where, trust me, the
house always cleans up.

As expected, we rocked the house that night with sets
that mixed in some of my early originals like "The Fall" and
"My Friend" with a healthy assortment of our strongest, most
crowd-pleasing covers like Van Morrison's "Brown Eyed Girl,"
the Meters' "Hey Pocky A-Way," Ray Charles' "Hit the Road

Jack," the Temptations' "Ain't Too Proud to Beg," and maybe an Elton John or Billy Joel tune thrown in every once in a while to mellow things out if the room got too rowdy.

After the show, the owner burst into our room with a big grin on his face and told us, "We all had a *great* night." He then quickly handed me a bag with what we thought was all our money. And the strange thing was, this bag looked as if somebody had already gone through it more times than if it were suspicious luggage at the airport. Instantly, I knew that *somebody* at the club had already gone through that bag—our piece of the night's big action—and decided to make an exceptionally generous donation to themselves.

I remember hurriedly counting out the total take for the night in front of the guys—in the bag was less than $600! We were all furious. Most nights, $600 would have been a mother lode—more than enough for gas and food and maybe even a little lodging or other luxury. But this was our *big* night—our huge football weekend score—and it pissed us off no end that someone else had helped themselves to what was rightfully *our* money.

Since we were the Taylor Hicks Band and for better or worse, I was Taylor Hicks, I was the one who had to step up and do something quick. So I ran right back to confront the owner. I found the bastard still grinning and told him, "We're *not* idiots. We *know* you took our money."

Normally, this was the classic kind of argument you can't win. As in a Las Vegas casino, in the clubs it's almost impossible to beat the house, especially because you're on their turf and they have security on their side. I might have just let it go, but as we stood there backstage screaming at each other—with the crowd still happily milling around and racking up bar tabs out front—I noticed that the owner still had one of *our* hundred-dollar bills sticking out of the pocket of his jeans. Afraid or just embarrassed, the jerk told me to come back to his office and he'd give me the rest of our money. In that moment, I wasn't sure if I was going to be paid or killed, but the prospect of the first option was appealing enough to overlook the risk of the second.

What happened next, I have to admit, gave me the sweetest pleasure. Just as this gentleman—and I use the term loosely—was walking through the kitchen toward his back office, he suddenly slipped on the wet floor and fell loudly and painfully on his hip. I'll never forget the sight of him crawling back to his desk, writhing in pain and reluctantly pulling the rest of our money out of a drawer. I don't think of myself as a particularly cruel man, but sometimes club owners *are* thieving bastards, and sometimes karma *is* a bitch.

Keeping things together on the road was never easy. I took many wrong turns and got lost many nights. One night, on my way to Destin, Florida, we got so lost we just ended up eating on the road and driving right back home, never even making the gig. Sometimes the tension in the van was unbearable. There were countless times when our petty disputes almost came to blows, but fortunately, I always had a tire tool handy. Somewhere along the way, I'd found the tool to be useful for calming down a disgruntled musician. Leading a band can be like captaining a ship. Sometimes the only justice you have time for is rough justice. If, for example, a guy shirked his band obligations to shack up with some girl, he might find himself left behind.

For a long while, my dream booking was a Friday night gig before the big Alabama-Tennessee football game. But whenever I called to plead our case, every place was always already booked. The other big score I constantly dreamed of—in terms of image, at least—was getting selected as the opening act for the national acts that would come through the area. I remember doing everything imaginable to secure a spot opening a local show for Widespread Panic, whose music we'd played in Passing Through.

No matter what I said or did, the promoter kept telling me, "*Can't* do it. It's called 'An Evening with Widespread Panic.'" See, when you hear the phrase "An Evening with . . . ," that means that whoever's name follows doesn't want an opening act. To me, "An Evening with . . ." came to mean "An Evening *Without* Taylor Hicks." I must have heard that same excuse from promoters a million times over the years, but it never went down well. When you come see me in concert, I promise to give you an evening—*and* an opening act.

I could never afford to be too proud. If I had to stand

naked on Main Street for ten days to get a gig, I'd do it. If you don't have anybody else working to promote you, you can't be shy about promoting yourself. There's a very fine line between a pain in the ass and a highly motivated individual, and I know I crossed that line plenty of times. If I had a dollar for every time I snuck around a town late at night putting up posters of myself for some bar gig, I'd be a lot better off today.

When you're trying to make it big, you can't be shy about letting people know who you are or what you do. Most probably won't care, but a few will, and a couple of those people might even like you and spread the word. Fame is a numbers game, and on your way up, you have to do whatever it takes to get yourself in front of as many people as possible.

Once in a great while, somebody in a position to help would actually say yes and give me a chance. Thanks to those people, I had the experience and honor of opening for everybody from James Brown to Jackson Browne, both of whom, incidentally, were nice enough to say hi to me backstage.

Opening for much bigger and better-known acts was an education in and of itself. As an opener, you learn how to grab an audience right out of the gate and make an impression—because if you don't, you'll have to learn a much more painful lesson: namely, how to dodge fruit, vegetables, and the occasional beer can.

I still remember the pure, funky thrill of being told, "Okay, Taylor, shut up, you *can* open for James Brown and do the Jubilee City Fest." There was no negotiating on a plum gig like that. This was one of the times I was told right up front that we wouldn't get paid a cent. But who cared? To share a bill with James Brown, I'd work pro bono. To make the offer even more appetizing, we were informed there'd be free Coca-Cola backstage because the company was sponsoring the event. If we were lucky, there might even be a few free salads backstage that we could help ourselves to after we played.

How did I feel about playing my heart out for soda and salad? I felt *good*—to borrow a phrase from the Godfather of Soul himself. That day I remember thinking that James Brown looked *exactly* like James Brown—all dressed up, still looking fine, with his teeth shining in the sun. I was truly honored to be in the Godfather's presence.

With the work ethic I'd inherited from the Hicks family, I respected the hardest-working man in show business as much as anyone. As I write these words, the world has just lost Mr. Brown, so I feel especially privileged to have had the chance to share a stage with the man himself. I would have *paid* to play that night.

In the music business it doesn't take long to discover that a lot of people are full of hot air. For reasons that elude me, a lot of people in power can't wait for a chance to pop your balloon along the way. Then you come across the real deal and see how it *should* be done. I'll be forever thankful that I got to share time on the road with some of the music greats who blazed the trail for the rest of us to follow.

Over the years, the Taylor Hicks Band was also honored to open for some of the most exciting *younger* acts out there today—great artists like Robert Randolph, who's one of the guitar gods worth worshiping, and the modern bluesman Keb' Mo', who'd become a friend and, as I'll describe later, helped me *not* give up during one of my darkest days.

Those were our red-letter days—the very rare glamour gigs. Still, there was nothing fancy about most of the places the band played or the way we lived. We traveled light and ate cheap out of necessity, not choice. Our path was rarely an easy one.

That said, I remain very proud to have cut my teeth as a performer at some of those less than glamorous southern joints long referred to as the chitlin' circuit. When I say chitlin' circuit, I'm talking about the same sort of down-home, fantastically greasy southern clubs and roadhouses where great artists like my hero Ray Charles and the Ike and Tina Turner Revue and countless other R&B greats played once upon a time.

The world around these great old joints has changed a good deal over the years, but you'd be surprised to learn that some of those places have somehow managed to stay the same. Sure, they might try changing the oil in their fry cookers every ten years or so, but often that's pretty much it as far as change goes.

Some of the places we played could get a little rough. Nothing much was sugarcoated there except maybe the sweet pastries behind the bar that we'd try to get the waitresses to sneak us for free. Let me tell you, there's nothing remotely glitzy about life on the chitlin' circuit. In such joints you're highly unlikely to get spotted by Simon Cowell, Paula Abdul, or even Randy Jackson, but you'll find some of the most discerning and enthusiastic audiences there nonetheless.

Playing for a year on that kind of down-home road circuit taught me everything I ever *really* needed to know about how to work a crowd and build a set. The lessons I learned in those sweaty roadside clubs—often for close to no money and too many times in front of almost no people—are the same exact lessons that helped me capitalize on the biggest break imaginable when it came my way.

Playing the chitlin' circuit any chance we got—as well as any other club, frat party, or backyard BBQ that would have us—we learned the simple rule that I still live by to this very day: either you entertain people or you go home.

Whatever the venue, whatever the circumstances, your job is to do whatever you must to leave them cheering and begging for more. Over the years, I've entertained people amid truly bizarre and questionable circumstances—or nearly died trying. One time the band and I got hired to play a house auction. I still remember someone from the real estate company coming over to me while we were playing and telling me to turn the volume down whenever a serious bidder came forward. That's a tough gig.

Over the years, we played on every kind of stage—on

wood, on concrete, in a tree, and even on top of a pretty flimsy piece of plastic that somebody haphazardly slapped over a swimming pool. From the relative safety of the stage, I've seen plenty of fights break out and lots of bottles come flying in my general direction.

Experience has taught me the hard way that music can be a contact sport, especially at gigs like the Annual Interstate Mullet Toss, which is held each year at the fabulous Flora-Bama in Gulf Shores, Alabama. Trust me, you really *should* have been there, and if you *were* there, you—like me—probably don't remember much now. That gig was basically three days of sunburned Alabamans downing as much liquor as any human can consume. Throw in a lot of mullets and a couple of flirty girlfriends, and you've basically got the makings of a redneck Molotov cocktail, or what most people back home like to call "a real good time."

The road does offer a kind of freedom. In my case, it certainly wasn't financial freedom, but it was freedom all the same. Unfortunately, as I found when I was trying to get the Taylor Hicks Band off the ground, that kind of freedom can finally take its toll.

When you live mostly on the road, coming home to maybe do laundry and sleep for a couple of hours, there's precious little to ground you. Along the way, I was fortunate that a few sweet, smart women with big hearts were there in

Birmingham to give me a better reason to rush home. The women in my life back then were genuinely understanding. If they were going to be foolish enough to put up with me, they *had* to be understanding.

The lifestyle I was living then in no way lent itself to being a good boyfriend—or even, as I'd find out, a good person. For me, the bleakest times in my adult life—if you can really call it that—were the times I now refer to as "the asshole years." Please excuse my occasional cussing in this book. That too is part of my ugly truth—if you stay on the road long enough, you *will* start to talk like a trucker.

My own dismal dark ages were the years between twenty-five and twenty-eight, when pretty much nothing was going right. Revealingly, I think, the music I was making at the time wasn't very good either. During that time, my band became a real revolving door. You could hear the chaos in the music, and we became more and more unfocused. That, in turn, led to lots of clubs not wanting to book the band anymore. That lack of bookings led to almost no money coming in—which, of course, led to even more people leaving the band. For me, this was becoming an especially vicious circle.

Sadly, I reacted to it all by turning into a real prick for a stretch—a pretty long stretch, if I remember right. There are no good excuses for being a total jerk, but back then I do remember feeling weighed down by an array of problems. I needed money. I needed sleep. More than anything, I needed a big break—especially considering the growing pressure from my father, who logically kept telling me it was time to grow up, give up, and get a real job. I was scared my father was right.

Somewhere along the road, I'd lost my way. In fact, it's quite easy to lose your way on the road, and not just on the map. So many players get caught up in the partying. If you're not careful, you can find yourself forgetting about the one thing that put you on the road in the first place—the music— and replace it with people and substances that are threatening to your health and well-being.

That's a dangerous and even life-threatening mistake to make. My hero Ray Charles famously lost his way for many years, getting involved with hard drugs. Incredibly, he somehow still managed to keep working at a genius level for a long, long time. Sadly, the rest of us aren't gifted enough to pull off that trick.

In my life, I've been no angel. Spending as much time in bars as I have, I've seen it all and done it all. Okay, maybe I've haven't quite done it *all*, but I've done most of it—and undoubtedly a whole lot more than I really should have. For a consistently struggling D-list musician like I was in those days, getting drunk and messed up from time to time can come to seem like a pretty decent HMO plan. Life on the road comes to feel like a lonely struggle for survival. In your isolation and confusion, and faced with so much doubt and uncertainty, you can stupidly decide that medicating yourself is a good idea.

Getting high—with one substance or another—was one way of forgetting for a short time that I was a twenty-seven-year-old sleeping on some twenty-one-year-old girl's couch, playing beach bars for college boys and girls who'd shortly go back to their schools and graduate to something better, leaving me running in place.

I'm not proud of any of my dopey behavior, but when you're *living* the road musician lifestyle for a very long time, getting out of your own head can seem like the best option.

The songs I write come from my experiences—pleasant or otherwise. For example, I once wrote a song called "Macon County Blues" after I got popped on the interstate in Florida with some pot in my car. I'm not proud of that, but it's true—I *have* inhaled.

When it came time for my hearing, I walked into the courtroom and told the bailiff that if the great B. B. King could play Cook County Jail, then I guess I could pass a few hours in the Macon County Jail. Of course, B. B. King recorded a classic album in *his* penal facility, and I was just another dumb stoner screwing things up again. If nothing else, at least I made the bailiff laugh. For all my youthful trouble-making, I'm no experienced jailbird, but I figured if you can make the bailiff crack up, that's a good thing.

With no record deal, no representation, and no clear prospects of anything changing soon, I felt as though I had once and for all hit the end of the road. At twenty-seven, my life and my career had come down to driving five hundred miles to play a few nights in some town, then waking up on some strange chick's couch, usually with some other nasty band guys on the same floor. Beggars and bar singers can't be choosers. Typically, there were beer bottles everywhere and our host would have to leave early for work. She'd turn off the air-conditioning because she couldn't pay her bills, and the room would get as hot and sweaty and smelly as the van we now had to jump back into for the next long drive.

If you'd spotted me on one of those mornings, I'm sure you'd have pegged me as closer to forty-seven than twenty-seven. Truthfully, that kind of life has its moments, but give it time and it'll wear you out. There were too many mornings when I'd wake up not knowing where I was. Even once I got my bearings, there were plenty of times when I wondered what the hell I was doing there anyway.

We all get lost sometimes in our lives—that's part of being on a journey and being human. A wiser man than me, Henry David Thoreau, once wrote that it's not until we're lost that we begin to understand ourselves. For me, the real measure of a man isn't whether he gets lost but whether he can still manage to find his way back somehow.

Trying anything I could to find my way back—and maybe even do the right thing for once—I made a hard decision. The time had come to get off the road and give normal life at least one halfhearted chance.

8

THE WEDDING SINGER

I KNOW LOVE IS AROUND THE CORNER
AND HEARTACHE'S AROUND THE BEND
WHEN WILL THIS LASTING DARKNESS
EVER COME TO AN END?

—"Heart and Soul" by Taylor Hicks

As I'd done many times before, I woke up one morning in yet another college girl's trashed apartment in yet another unremarkable town. With sleep still in my eyes, I navigated my way around some of the boys in the band—at that moment passed out on the living room floor—searching for the nearest possible bathroom. The very last thing I wanted to do was awaken our generous and no doubt thoroughly hungover host.

Looking at my face in the mirror, I didn't like what I saw one bit. I looked like hell, which was about right considering that was exactly how I felt. Besides my now entirely gray hair, there were some new lines on my face that I hadn't spotted before. It may have been just the crappy lighting, but I felt certain it was the crappy living.

On a big, professional music tour—like the one I'd eventually go on after winning *American Idol* and, later, after releasing my first major label—the experience can be like living inside a very comfortable cocoon. Onstage you're exposed to your loving public for a couple of hours at night, but much of the rest of the day you're fairly protected, slightly coddled, and even downright pampered. It's good work if you can get it.

In contrast, when you're out on the road picking up stray gigs in random towns for what amounts to spare change, hauling your own beat-up gear and looking for free room and board whenever possible, there isn't any pampering whatsoever. If it weren't for the occasional kindness of strangers, you wouldn't even have a place to sleep most nights.

A lot of musicians like to think of themselves as gypsies by choice, a secret tribe that yearns for the supposedly careful life of a traveling minstrel. No matter what story they tell themselves, though, there comes a time when the whole act gets old. And that morning, as I beheld the scary sight of my tired old face, I realized I was getting old *quick*. For the life of me, I couldn't figure out where I was going next and why I was going there.

It was time to have a serious talk with myself. Thinking back on it, I'd done exactly what I promised I'd do when I returned from Nashville. I'd formed my own band and became a true road warrior on behalf of the soulful music that meant everything to me. Unfortunately, now—long after I'd assumed I'd be discovered—I was no better off. Once more, my plan was failing before my eyes. That road warrior I saw in the mirror looked very much like he was played out.

"What the hell are you *doing* with your life, Taylor?" my father had asked on more occasions than I cared to remember. Usually I dodged the question, responded with something like "I'm doing exactly what I want" or "Whatever it takes to make it, man." Now, after too many years spent trying to impress him and others by talking up my next big gig or that record deal I just *knew* was coming my way soon, I couldn't even *fake* optimism convincingly.

For five years now, I'd followed my burning passion for music wherever it led, and to appraising eyes like my father's, I had nothing much to show for it. I'd left college far behind, and with it anything remotely like a healthy lifestyle, a normal schedule, or predictable career path. I'd made my choice willingly and with total conviction that somehow it would all work out in the end. And despite every wrong turn I'd taken, I still believed I had a voice to share. As embarrassing as it sounds to say, I felt special, as if I were born for one purpose—to sing and entertain people who were going through their own journeys and troubles.

However, the old reliable *motivating* inner voices were now drowned out by other voices. We all have voices in our heads, and I think for many of us, the dominant ones are those of our parents. My mother's voice was about following my bliss, which turned out to be music. My father's voice, now the more dominant one, was one of serious and growing concern.

It all added up to a ton of self-doubt.

If you're going in the wrong direction, even if you're stubborn as hell, eventually you see that it's time to stop, pull off the road, and maybe even turn around. And so I decided it was time for another change in plans.

Famous bands break up; the Taylor Hicks Band just stopped trying for a while. Even if we had formally announced that we were splitting up, it's not exactly like *Rolling Stone* and *Spin* would have been fighting tooth and nail for the exclusive rights to the story. And so it was that, for a short while there in 2004, I actually tried out a real, almost legitimate job. By legitimate job, I mean any paying gig that didn't involve playing the harmonica or singing "In the Midnight Hour" sometime after one in the morning to a bunch of people who really ought to be going home.

I seem to remember around this time my father approaching me and suggesting I seriously consider a career in the growing field of prosthetics—which for some reason reminded me of Dustin Hoffman in *The Graduate* being pointed toward the exciting world of plastics. Not that I should have been turning down good advice. After all, unlike Dustin, I wasn't even a graduate.

Bottom line, though: for two of the longest and most grueling weeks in the history of the American workplace, I copped an attitude and picked up a check at a Birmingham nursing home, doing what was euphemistically referred to as "health services." It was a fancy job title that wrongly conjured up images of me saving lives and breaking hearts as a kind of white-haired Dr. McDreamy on a very special episode of *Grey's Anatomy*. What "health services" really meant was that it was my job to do whatever it was that nobody else on staff was willing to do. In other words, for a shameless showboat like me who'd gotten terribly spoiled living in the spotlight, this new job was anything but a big star turn.

At the nursing home, my primary responsibilities ended up being stripping and waxing floors and helping as best I could with building upkeep. After years spent traveling from town to town, taking in an ever-changing procession of people and places and playing music at all hours, usually to at least some modest reaction, I'd gotten very used to a certain amount of visual stimulation and direct feedback. Unfortunately, stimulation wasn't a big priority at the nursing home. I soon found myself overwhelmingly bored and every bit as tired as most of the residents—most of whom, unlike yours truly, had at least already lived full and productive lives.

Coming off the difficult-to-beat high of performing for people on a regular basis, I crashed down to earth pretty hard. It was almost as if the music were *literally* draining from my life. It felt as if some vital essence were escaping, leaving a husk in its place. Once again, my best-laid plans had gone awry.

Almost immediately upon getting the job, I began to dream up emancipation scenarios. My fantasy became that of getting fired. Unfortunately, getting anyone to notice me long enough to recognize my obvious failings proved surprisingly difficult. Despite my clearly second-rate work and transparently bad attitude, I still seemed to be in the running for the Employee of the Month Award.

Ultimately, salvation came in the form of a phone call from a woman asking me to play an unusually profitable wedding date. I did the math and immediately calculated that the amount of money I could make for putting on a tux and singing Kool and the Gang's "Celebration," "(I've Had) The Time of My Life" from *Dirty Dancing*, "Just the Way You Are" by Billy Joel, and a dozen other wedding-gig standards added up to as much as I'd make for two full weeks of hard labor at the nursing home.

So I thought long and hard—okay, maybe it was *short* and hard. Wouldn't *you* rather pass the time at a joyful celebration than push poor old ninety-something Ethel into the hall in preparation for stripping floors? Especially if the wedding gig pays a whole lot more? God help me, I was born to sing, not sweep.

When that day I happily tendered my resignation, I promised myself I'd work at a nursing home again only if it was as a singer—definitely not as a floor stripper. Strangely enough, I *would* work a few nursing-home singing gigs over the years. Being a gray-haired individual myself and having lots of songs in my repertoire that just *sounded* old, I tended to go down pretty well with my elders. Sadly, though, that kind of following tends to die off, so there wasn't much future in making nursing-home gigs my bread and butter.

Anyway, to my father's chagrin, and my incredible relief, I finally had the pleasure of failing at something other than making my name in music. This gave me the perfect cover to make my way back to music again. I'm lucky in a sense to have had a practical dad. When, later on, Dad heard about my trying out for *Idol,* the first thing he said was, "Oh, you're going to do *American Idol.* Why don't you just go buy a lottery ticket?" I'm certain it was unintentional, but by relentlessly hammering away at the importance of being practical, my dad ultimately drove me to *reject* practicality.

Reading that last line, I guess it can sound like I'm knocking my dad. But that isn't my point at all. Look, I understand that it was my dad's genetic mandate to steer his son down practical paths. That's what dads *do.* If dads stopped lecturing and ticking off the risks, there'd be a whole generation of twenty-something guys trying to make the Yankees or playing mean guitar in garage bands. The economy would grind to a halt. I *get* it. Still, I feel like I want to say something about this. I'm not a parent myself, so I'm really in no position to give any advice to parents, but what the heck, I'll give it a shot anyway.

Please, if you do have kids, don't spend all of your time simply worrying about their futures. Every once in a while, take the time to actually *listen* to your kids' dreams, and maybe even try believing in those dreams too. The truth is, you never know when one might come true.

Having thankfully gotten out of that nursing home alive— and lest you forget, not everybody *does*—I became for a short time your quintessential wedding singer. I hope my tuxedos were slightly more tasteful than Adam Sandler's in that very funny movie of the same name, but I couldn't swear to it. I do know that, working as a wedding singer, I never picked up a girl as adorable as Drew Barrymore.

In all candor, there were more than a few times during my stint as a wedding sensation that I would have preferred to be hanging back with Ethel at the nursing home. Weddings may be the happiest day in the lives of the bride and groom—the jury's still out on that one—but they're often precisely the opposite for the wedding singer and bandleader. After all, unlike Vince Vaughan and Owen Wilson in that other funny movie, the guy behind the microphone is there to get paid not laid, and working the ballrooms can be much more complicated than you might think.

Seeking to at least look like a professional, I put together a relatively well-kempt group of musicians who could play the jazzy blues sound that seems to go down well at weddings. Before very long, we vaguely resembled and even sounded a lot like one of your top-notch wedding bands. And yet, even though the gigs generally paid quite well and usually got booked far enough in advance to make it easier to find downtime, I still had a lot of issues with the job.

Here's how it typically went wrong. Usually the bride and groom are the ones who book you, and usually they're all excited and happy to have you around. Then on the big wedding day, the bride and groom are off taking pictures. Suddenly, out of nowhere you're dealing with the bride's mom or maybe the dad, who's the one who's actually supposed to pay you. Inevitably, both parents become vocal about their musical preferences. For example, freaked out by the pressures of the event, the mom may cuss at you because she can't fathom why on earth you can't play more Frank Sinatra instead of all that loud Motown material. So then you play "It Had to Be You" just as close as you can to how Ol' Blue Eyes did it, and just as that winds down the bride's grandmother slowly makes her way over and starts rolling her eyes because *she* wants more Glenn Miller big band numbers and please not so much of that Sinatra stuff.

So now you get your band cranked up to play Glenn Miller's "In the Mood." And just as you're making your little band sound as big as humanly possible, the groom's cool young cousin rushes to the stage. This guy loudly and drunkenly demands you play "Been Caught Stealing" by Jane's Addiction, or something else so wildly inappropriate that it constitutes clear musical malpractice for any working wedding band. Finally, there's a whole interfamily trickle-down effect because now the bride's dad appears, upset because his wife is thinking you ought to go back and play more of that Motown stuff that had all the young people dancing.

That, my friends, is exactly how somebody else's big blessed event becomes a pain in the ass for you, the wedding singer. Based on my extensive experience, here is my two cents for arranging the music for your wedding: please, by all means, hire a good DJ. Unlike me, DJs love taking request after request.

My own childhood didn't leave me with the most positive view of matrimony, but I don't think that's why I ultimately wanted to divorce myself from the wedding band world. It had more to do with the lack of musical input.

Whenever I played in clubs, I always sang cover versions of great songs, along with songs of my own. I never resented singing other people's hits—especially since I had none of my own. Hell, I love the great old songs as much as the next guy—even *more*, really. But as time went on, music got to be way too personal a thing for me to feel satisfied just being a human jukebox and playing whatever struck someone's else's fancy. Furthermore, despite loving a good celebration as much as anyone, I happen to sing "Celebration" really, *really* badly.

Still, the wedding band shows served their purpose. After a month or two of having been out of the game—and suffering from resulting symptoms of harmonica withdrawal—I started to feel the old musical spark again.

Playing my first post-Ethel wedding gradually led to

more and more work. Bar mitzvah gigs, of which I also played a few, were a little better. Frat party gigs were still a whole lot of fun—sometime *too much* fun. There, you had an energetic audience that was expressly there to party. Plus, the money is typically guaranteed, and those eternally youthful college girls are always present and plentiful. I suppose that when your work isn't making you rich, you might as well savor whatever fringe benefits exist.

I eventually decided, though, that the frat life wasn't good for my spirit—or body. There were a lot of great frat nights—and a lot of decidedly *less* great frat mornings when the bands and I would wake up in the same venue, our path to the exit blocked by beer bottles and other dangerous obstacles. As the morning unwound, most of the frat boys and girls would head off to the library, and we'd get right back on the interstate and hit the Waffle House. Unfortunately, that sort of fun—and food—will catch up to you eventually.

So I finally started to clean up my act. I began consuming somewhat better food and a lot less of other substances that could potentially kill me. With a partially restored metabolism, my ambition swelled. I decided to take one more shot—maybe one *last* shot—at tracking down that ever-elusive major-label record contract. For a second time, I decided to invest my own money—plus whatever other funds I could beg, borrow or steal from my family—and record my own album.

This time "good" wouldn't be good enough. I pulled

together the strongest lineup of musicians I'd ever had. My trusty friend John Cook played guitar, as did myself and Wynn Christian, who added some fine electric work too. Mitch Jones, on bass, and Patrick Lunceford, on drums, were my rock-solid rhythm section. Last but hardly least, Brian Less, on piano and Hammond B3 organ, brought a whole lot of soul to the proceedings. Bands either have chemistry or not, and during the few hours we could afford in the studio, we definitely had it.

Somehow, for a little more than $4,500, I managed to produce seven tracks of which I'm still extremely proud. To me, the result sounded like a million bucks—or at the very least, say, $250,000. In hopes of finally changing my luck, I named the album *Under the Radar*. I was betting everything that the music on it would lift me up and finally put me on the map.

Under the Radar kicked off with "The Deal," a romantic midtempo number that had become a big live-audience favorite, and was a song I'd revisit years later. For my money—and it *was* my money—there were two other real standouts on *Under the Radar*.

"Hell of a Day" was based on an expression I remember my grandfather Earl favoring when I was little. By now, Earl had died of cancer, but his warmth and low-key way of comforting me would never be forgotten. Often Grandpa would talk about how it had been a hell of a day at work, but one day I realized that you could have a hell of a day in *love* too. I felt my song captured that feeling.

For my money, the other standout track on *Under the Radar* was a song titled "Soul Thing." To this day, "Soul Thing" is as close as I've come to writing a personal anthem. I love everything about the song because it's extremely true to who I am and where I've been. You can definitely hear strong echoes of my own brush with Nashville in the song's chorus:

> It ain't no groove thing
> It ain't no country twang,
> It's a simple refrain;
> It's a soul thing.

As with "The Deal," I'd later make the decision to re-record "Soul Thing" for my major-label debut after becoming an American Idol. But when I recorded "Soul Thing" originally, there was no big record contract in sight. So my band and I hit the road as much as possible to try to spread the word.

As work increased for us again around the South, the band got better and better. My "asshole years" became a distant memory, and I realized that, after about ten years of grinding things out, the music was actually sounding good, even *great* on our best nights. We started building an impressive following—at least, on the scale these things are measured.

Around the time we finished *Under the Radar,* there were

a number of little markets where we were doing quite well—places like Auburn, Tuscaloosa, and a number of hot spots alongside the coast. Apparently, the Taylor Hicks Band was getting known as the life of any beach party.

Nashville was still very tough for us to crack, but Atlanta was getting better and better. We even started to make small inroads outside the Southeast. For instance, we got to play Café Boogaloo in Hermosa Beach, California, and we did the little room at the House of Blues in Los Angeles, right on the Sunset Strip.

As if that weren't enough, we even got to play a corporate function at the Playboy Mansion. From one perspective, a hormonally charged one, this was the single most exciting gig any red-blooded American band could play. From another, it was just another gig. The reality of playing the Mansion is that you're among the Bunnies not as an honored guest but as hired help. In other words, Hef's got it covered, boys . . . leave your bathrobe at home.

I must confess, though: loading our equipment in and out of the Playboy Mansion was a blast because of the occasional glimpses it afforded of Playmate skin.

Besides checking out the gorgeous view from the Playboy Mansion, we'd come to Los Angeles on a mission to get *Under the Radar* into the hands of the right people—ones who might at long last sign us up. Years earlier, that A&R man in Nashville had told me that if I was ever going to find my record deal, I needed to look in Los Angeles. Now I was banking on his being right. The way the guys and I saw it, the songs were there, the band was ready, and it was time for the Taylor Hicks Band to finally collect our gold and platinum rewards.

But just like that great line in "Lullaby" by Shawn Mullins, Los Angeles turned out to be "kind of like Nashville with a tan." All these years after Nashville's country labels had passed on me because I didn't fit into their country playbook, Los Angeles' rock and pop labels told me I didn't fit into their playbooks either. The bottom line was that I just didn't fit in *anywhere*—either rock, pop, or country. I was a man without a genre, and once again without any real prospects. In other words, "Thanks, Taylor, but no thanks." We'd done our best, and somehow it still wasn't considered good enough.

During that period, I was staying at a self-consciously groovy L.A. hotel next to an even hipper bar where one night I ran into Dierks Bentley—the very cool country singer-songwriter who was then just beginning to make noise. Dierks has gone on to enjoy a nice run of country hits like "What Was I Thinkin'," "Come a Little Closer," and "Every Mile a Memory." He even won the very prestigious Horizon Award at the 2005 Country Music Association Awards. Dierks and I had some friends in common, and we'd both moved to Nashville right around the same time to try to make it in the music business there. Now, here *he* was right next to me living the dream, and here *I* was handing him my little press kit like the loser I was. He wished me luck, and I think we both knew I'd need it.

I remember thinking that night, as Dierks and I shot the breeze about his record deal, promotional tour, and video shoot, what a really wonderful guy he seemed to be and how all this good fortune really couldn't have befallen a nicer or more deserving fellow. I also thought, *Why the hell can't this be happening to me?* For the record, I didn't necessarily think those thoughts in exactly that order.

One of the most important emotional turning points in my life came on the day of Ray Charles' funeral.

There'd been a big music festival in Birmingham called City Stages at which all kinds of well-known bands and street bands played. It was there that I really got to hang with Keb' Mo'—also known as Kevin Moore—who is one of the best and most popular acoustic blues musicians around. We'd actually met in New Orleans three years before, and of course I handed him my music, looking for his opinion and his help.

Over time, Kevin and I became friendly—and when he played the Alabama Theater in Birmingham with the great singer-songwriter John Prine, I happily went to see the show, wearing some old shorts and looking like a slob. That night I was shocked when, in front of my hometown crowd, Kevin pulled me onstage with him and Prine. Of course, it doesn't take a lot to encourage me to take the stage, and that sort of public show of support meant the world to me.

Not long after that, my hero Ray Charles died. Even though I'd never met the man, when he passed I was utterly devastated. I decided to spend the Friday of the funeral around my computer screen listening to National Public Radio's live coverage of the ceremony at the First African Methodist Episcopal Church. In some small way, I wanted to pay my respects.

I'm glad I did listen to the event because Ray's funeral rightly featured some of the most moving music I've ever heard. The church's kids' choir sang the first part of the service. Glen Campbell sang "Where Should I Go but unto the Lord." Willie Nelson sang "Georgia on My Mind." Stevie Wonder sang too, and Wynton Marsalis played "Somewhere Over the Rainbow."

Sitting there in my little apartment listening to this historic event was one of the most powerful musical experiences of my life. I tell you, it was moving: all these musical legends, stripped down and at the height of their powers, paying their respects to a fallen giant. That day, you could pretty much stick a fork in me because I was *done.* Emotionally, I was probably in the worst shape I'd been in a long time. I just remember sitting there drowning in my tears.

As fate would have it, my dad happened to stop by that day—yes, that same messy-looking place you later saw on *American Idol* when the show came to town to film. When

Dad walked in, he couldn't understand what was going on. He started saying, "Taylor, what the hell are you *doing*? Why are you crying about Ray Charles? It's Friday and you should be going to work somewhere. You should be getting a real job, boy. You didn't even *know* Ray Charles!"

With that, he stormed out.

Listen, I understand that my dad was just worried about me. Hell, *I* was worried about me. But at that particular moment, all my father's words did was pour salt in a big open wound. No matter how confident or determined you might be, there are going to be moments when you hit bottom. This, for me, was one of those moments—and one I'll never forget.

Just as I'd hit my lowest point of the day, my phone rang. On the other end of the line was Keb' Mo', who, it turned out, was in my neck of the woods. I told him a little about what was going on. Kevin just said, "Come on, man, I'm picking you up and taking you to lunch." A few minutes later, he pulled up in his tour bus and rescued me from my misery.

Over our meal that day, I remember looking across the table at Kevin and asking, "What's it all about, man? How do you *do* it? How do you get to that place in your life where good things can happen?" To me, these were *the* questions, and I needed an answer right then and there. Kevin just sat there eating his pumpkin pie and finally pointed up to the sky with a big smile on his face. That was good enough for me.

Having this great, deeply soulful musician on my side that day made all the difference. For me, Kevin's being there to lift me up was one of those fortunate coincidences—those God-given little signs of hope—that manage to keep you going.

9

A CHANGE IN THE
WEATHER

IT'S BEEN A LONG, A LONG TIME COMING

BUT I KNOW A CHANGE IS GONNA COME, OH YES IT WILL.

—"A Change Is Gonna Come" by Sam Cooke

Unlike another well-known southern character, Blanche DuBois in Tennessee Williams' *A Streetcar Named Desire,* I haven't *always* depended on the kindness of strangers. I only started counting on strangers once I found my way onto *American Idol* and began trying to win over the American people as best I could. Rather, like a lot of people, I've always relied on the kindness, generosity, and understanding of my *friends.*

Throughout my life—especially when I've had family issues to contend with—I've leaned on good buddies of both sexes in countless ways. That was true back when I was a kid, and it's still true today. Having never settled down enough to start a family, I've looked instead to friends to keep me at least slightly grounded. These guys and gals were the first to notice me, look after me, give a damn about me. I guess you could call them my very first Soul Patrol.

Looking back now, I can see that I haven't always been a particularly easy friend to have either. I've asked much of my buddies, and I don't just mean pestering them to come to my gigs to make all those empty rooms feel a little more crowded. Along the way, I've borrowed money, crashed on couches, sat down at dining room tables uninvited, missed birthday parties, and generally been a pain.

Struggling and flailing around as much as I have, I've needed every friend willing to lend a hand. And so, in the thirteen unlucky months before opportunity really knocked for me, I was devastated when I lost not one but *three* good friends who, each in his own way, had helped me make it as far as I had. I learned the hard way that you should fully appreciate your friends while they're around.

I lost two of my buddies, Robert Hawkins and Dylan Berry, in separate car crashes. My third fallen friend, Jay Pearson—who will always be just J.P. to me—perished in a skiing accident.

The first of my friends to pass, Robert Hawkins, died in a car accident on the way to see a show I was promoting back in Birmingham. Robert owned a restaurant in town called the Open Door Café, a really great place that, true to its name, was a warm and welcoming spot where I could catch a brew, grab a meal, and find a smiling face or two even when I wasn't performing there. Robert was a sweet, fun-loving, and generous guy who always believed I'd make it one day. Whenever I was looking particularly down and defeated, he'd cheer me up by loudly playing Joe Walsh's "Life's Been Good" over the Open Door's sound system. Just like Robert himself, that song never failed to pick my mood right up.

The night Robert died I was at another bar in town watching a band play when we got the news that he'd been killed on his way to see the show. There was absolutely no way to make sense of it, then or now. Robert was way, way too young to leave this earth. But before he left, he definitely helped me see life's silver linings. When I think of him now, I think of his big smile. I *still* feel him smiling down at me.

Dylan Berry was another of my guardian angels. He was my childhood sweetheart's older brother and a couple of years older than me in school. Dylan was there when I was just beginning to explore music and figure out how to play it with other people. Truth is, he was always a little mad at me because I could play guitar a bit better than he could. He ended up becoming a great mandolin player instead. We'd sit around together and play songs and I always felt he had the perfect musical outlook. As things turned out, we didn't get to spend nearly enough time together, but I'll always remember Dylan as a kindred soul.

I remember I was playing at the Flora-Bama down on Gulf Shores around the July Fourth weekend when I got the call that Dylan and his wife had been involved in a horrible car accident and had both died. Thankfully, their son, Zeke, was saved. He's an awesome little dude now, living with Dylan's sister. I'm so grateful Zeke lives on to carry on the memory of his mom and dad. The funeral was, of course, a horribly painful but still deeply *spiritual* event for those who were there. I'll never forget when they played "Will the Circle Be Unbroken." The question the song asks never seemed quite as relevant before. To me, it's always seemed that, in our most heartbroken and desperate moments, music has unique power to start the healing process. This was one of those times.

Before J.P. died in such a shocking and sudden way while skiing, he gave me a book that really spoke to me. It was called *The Seat of the Soul* and was written by Gary Zukav, a Harvard graduate and Green Beret. In the book, Zukav—whom you might have seen on Oprah's show talking about *The Dancing Wu Li Masters: An Overview of the New Physics* or one of his other books—argues that we're evolving into multisensory organisms.

Zukav explains that humans are on a path toward having a much stronger and more sensitive sixth sense. He uses quantum physics—and lots of other things I never quite got around to mastering in high school—to show that we're all connected on a deeper level. As I interpret him, Zukav believes we can cultivate a bigger and better sixth sense if we recognize that potential within ourselves and work toward growing it. These days, I'll confess, I don't devote much time to exercising my sixth sense, but I do believe such a thing exists. I *know* it because I've felt it myself.

A Change in the Weather

My friend J.P. seemed to have a sixth sense about *me*. He always told me things were going to happen for me—that I shouldn't waste time doubting myself. While others were advising me to change careers—to consider selling prosthetics, for example—Jay was encouraging me to press on. Repeatedly, he told me I was going to catch a break and that I should never sell my dream short. He believed in me even when I began to doubt myself.

Many times J.P. would say, "Man, you're going to be a star someday." When he died, I was out on the road playing another show in another town and couldn't even begin to process the devastating loss. Finally, a couple of days later, I was able to make it to our friend Ray's house so we could talk about what had happened and comfort each other. I walked outside that night and looked up toward the heavens—searching for answers, I guess. Wouldn't you know it, the first thing I spotted in the night sky was a beautiful blazing shooting star.

I believe in signs. I believe they're all around us if only our eyes are open to see them. And I *definitely* believe in karma and a higher power. In this life, we all need buddies like mine—friends who believe in us early and often, the kind of true pals who stand by our side even when there's a price to pay for doing so. *That's* the sort of entourage we all need in our lives. My friends inspire me in death, just as they did in life.

Robert's, Dylan's, and J.P.'s deaths were a sudden and shocking loss for their families and for all who loved them dearly. I'll never forget any one of them, *ever,* no matter what happens in my life. Their deaths at such ridiculously early ages are a painful reminder that none of us is promised *anything*—not even a full thirty years of chasing one's dream.

In the end, losing so many friends in such a short time reinforced my faith rather than destroyed it. I believe in my heart that my friends are all angels now—angels who are still there pushing me on from above. I think of them all the time.

By the way, on the subject of God, faith, angels, and all that, I don't mean to imply that some heavenly script called for me to achieve the success I ultimately did. I don't think God worries too much about *American Idol* vote tallies. And besides, let's be real here: I've spent significantly more time in bars than in churches. Yet I do talk to God from time to time. Those conversations are personal, so I won't reveal them in these pages. But I *can* say that they've helped me to keep on keeping on.

I believe having a spiritual side makes you a better person, and by extension a better singer. Study music history as I have and you'll see that a lot of the greatest singers walked the line between the roadhouse and the church, the profane and the sacred, the sin of Saturday night and the salvation of Sunday morning. People like Johnny Cash, Sam Cooke, and Al Green negotiated that line with amazing grace.

What's sometimes forgotten is that there are deep feelings and real emotion in the music of church. Singing is all about conveying emotion and stirring something in others—and that happens only if the message you're sharing is coming

Clockwise, from top left: Me at age three. Though some of my best memories as a kid are of Christmas, most of the time comfort and joy were hard to come by. ♪ That's me *(on the right)* and a buddy at New Orleans' Jackson Square, two decades before Hurricane Katrina altered my musical destiny. ♪ There were good times watching college football with my dad. Here I am at age fourteen, hoping for gridiron glory. ♪ Basketball was actually my better sport, but at age eighteen I was already dreaming of making music—even if I didn't exactly look the part. ALL PHOTOGRAPHS COURTESY OF BRAD HICKS

Clockwise from top left: My friend J.P. *(middle)* believed in me when almost no one else did. He kept telling me I'd make it big someday. After he died in a skiing accident, I thought often of our friendship and his encouraging words. My guitarist at the time, Jon Cook, is pictured on the right. ♩ While matriculating at Auburn University, I seized on any opportunity to *not* hit the books, which turned out to be very unlucky for one particular fish. ♩ Though my dad rolled his eyes at my dreams of being a singer, he was always there for me. So was my grandmother Jonie, from whom I learned some of the marketing tricks that would serve me well on the road and, later, competing on *American Idol.* ALL PHOTOGRAPHS COURTESY OF BRAD HICKS

My second independent album, *Under the Radar,* which I produced myself, was supposed to be my ticket to fame. But fame decided to postpone its arrival. COURTESY OF TAYLOR HICKS

You'll notice that among *American Idol*'s Season #5 Top 12 finalists there's only one with gray hair. I figured that sticking out like a sore thumb might actually be an advantage. I'm in the middle, with *(from left to right)* Bucky Covington, Kellie Pickler, Paris Bennett, Lisa Tucker, Kevin Covais, Melissa McGhee, Ace Young, Mandisa Hundley, and Katharine McPhee. Elliott Yamin and Chris Daughtry are kneeling in front. VINCE BUCCI/GETTY IMAGES

At the point I was one of only three remaining contestants on *Idol,* there was a celebration in my honor in my hometown of Birmingham. Here you can see me from the back as I raise my arms in triumph. All the while I was thinking, *Is this really happening?* BUTCH DILL/ ASSOCIATED PRESS

For my final performances on *American Idol,* I decided to break out my secret weapon: the infamous "purple jacket." All over America, people were adjusting the color on their TV sets.
VINCE BUCCI/GETTY IMAGES

Left: For complicated reasons, growing up with my mom was nothing like a happy family sitcom. I know she was always pulling for me, though, and I've probably inherited from her my wanderlust and fun-loving ways. Here she is in the center of a viewing party at the Birmingham Jefferson Convention Complex right after I won the *Idol* contest. ♪ *Right:* A camera panning that same party shows all the affection I received from my hometown. It was an overwhelming display of support for which I'll always be deeply grateful. BOTH PHOTOGRAPHS ROB CARR/ASSOCIATED PRESS

Opposite: Here I am at the precise moment I realized I'd won. Ryan Seacrest *(left)* and my co-finalist Katharine McPhee seem almost as excited. VINCE BUCCI/GETTY IMAGES

Me again, hamming it up with Katharine, who was a good sport through it all.

How many entertainers have fantasized about someday appearing on *The Tonight Show*? Count me among them. Trading jokes with Jay Leno was a surreal moment.

On the *Idol* tour bus, things sometimes got heated as we separately plotted our post-*Idol* careers, but we had some goofy, fun moments, too. *Left to right:* Elliott, me, and Ace on the sofa, with Chris and Bucky in front of us. COURTESY OF TAYLOR HICKS

To Taylor Hicks
With best wishes,

Owing to the kindness of a special former teacher of mine, Susan Whitson, who wound up working for First Lady Laura Bush, I got to meet the president and hand him a "Soul Patrol" T-shirt. As far as *Idol* perks go, it doesn't get better than that. COURTESY OF TAYLOR HICKS

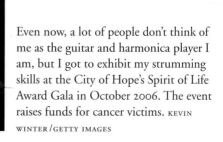

Even now, a lot of people don't think of me as the guitar and harmonica player I am, but I got to exhibit my strumming skills at the City of Hope's Spirit of Life Award Gala in October 2006. The event raises funds for cancer victims. KEVIN WINTER/GETTY IMAGES

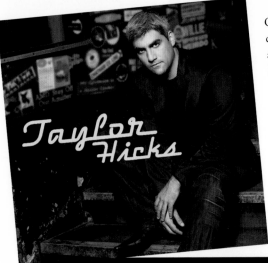

On December 12, 2006, my biggest dream came true when I had my first major-label album release, *Taylor Hicks*. Featuring songs I'd written myself, like "Soul Thing" and "The Deal," and others by top songwriters, the album ultimately went platinum, shipping more than a million copies. COURTESY OF TAYLOR HICKS

Above: As I've left *American Idol* behind and shaped a career that draws on my roots as a singer who loves to entertain live, it's been a thrill to perform with so many music legends, including Willie Nelson, the Allman Brothers, Widespread Panic, and, pictured here at the 2007 Orange Bowl, Gladys Knight. ELIOT SCHECHTER/GETTY IMAGES ♫ *Right:* Here I am in New Orleans, back where, in a sense, it all started. It was nearly being swept away by Hurricane Katrina that led to my attending the Las Vegas audition for *American Idol*. A year and a half later, I returned as the Mardi Gras Grand Marshal and reflected on how unpredictable, and wonderful, life can be— as long as you don't give up. COURTESY OF TAYLOR HICKS

from the heart *and* soul. In church music, you as a vocalist become a vehicle for the Holy Spirit. When many of the countless great church singers moved on to the more secular world—I'm thinking here of people like Sam Cooke after his early gospel recordings with the Soul Stirrers, or Aretha Franklin after she crossed over to pop and soul stardom—they took something holy and higher along with them. I believe they also took a seriousness of feeling and an ability to testify. No doubt they figured singing secular songs was just another way to spread a healing gospel.

Myself, I've felt the Spirit—or at least *a* spirit—move through me onstage, even when I've been playing some very ungodly clubs. When you think about it, the people in those beer-soaked clubs are a lot like the people sitting in church pews. They're all looking for something to lift them up and get them through another hard day and long night. Churches and gin mills are both places where people in need come in search of something to keep them going. Of course, the bar crowds do tend to get rowdier, but you get the idea.

The singers I admire most—the great soul singers—all sang songs of love, faith, and inspiration and always left people feeling a little better when they were done. You felt the pain and vulnerability in their voices, and yet their words somehow brought you joy and strength. As a philosopher once said, what doesn't kill us makes us stronger. I think my experiences with death just made me dig deeper and sing in a way that has helped me connect. Being so close to tragedy—and

living to tell—reminded me in the most powerful way that
life is *not* a dress rehearsal for those of us fortunate enough to
still be here living it.

Soon after losing my friends, I witnessed again the mysterious ways in which God works.

When Hurricane Katrina hit the Gulf Coast in August
2005, the storm and its aftermath killed many and devastated
countless lives. That the very same storm also wound up changing *my* life forever in a very different and utterly unexpected
way is proof that real life truly is stranger than fiction.

By a remarkable coincidence, Tracy—a wonderful female
friend of mine from college who lived in the same apartment
complex as most of my old bandmates in Passing Through—
was getting married in New Orleans to a great guy named
Brian Grubb on the very same weekend Katrina hit. Back
then, New Orleans truly was the Big Easy, a unique and often
carefree place. As a lover of fine music and food, I'd already
made New Orleans one of my favorite spots, and I welcomed
the chance to spend more time there. Unfortunately, perhaps
because of the city's caliber of musicians, it was hard for an
unknown like me to get invited there for a gig. But the next
best excuse to visit had to be going to a friend's wedding.

On Thursday I took a thirty-minute plane trip on Southwest that set me back a grand total of $75. And from the
moment my plane landed, I had a wonderful time, as people

tend to do when they go to New Orleans. Because of the music, the energy, and the vibe, and especially that Cajun food, the town is simply unbeatable. I'd brought along a girlfriend for the weekend, and the two of us decided to wake up Friday morning and walk around Jackson Square in the French Quarter. Later, we had dinner at Dickie Brennan's Steakhouse on Royal Street—an amazing white-tablecloth type of joint. At the time, we'd already heard there was a big storm coming up the Gulf, but nobody seemed terribly worried, at least not yet.

The church wedding at the Academy of the Sacred Heart Chapel on Saturday couldn't have been more gorgeous. The whole ceremony unfolded like in a dream, lit by the exquisite natural light of the Louisiana sunshine. Subsequently, I've been told that before a giant storm like Katrina, everything in the air gets sucked toward where the storm is and things get incredibly clear. The air feels purer and the natural light grows noticeably more intense. Perhaps that's the "calm before the storm" we've all heard so much about? Well, I'm here to say it's true; at least it was that day. For whatever reasons, everything looked absolutely heavenly inside the Catholic Church where we were gathered for Tracy and Brian. Not only was the bride glowing, so was the whole chapel.

Before the big wedding reception, I went back to the hotel. That's when I heard that Hurricane Katrina was now a Category 5 storm and that it was going to hit the area sometime Sunday morning.

I remember walking by Dickie Brennan's Steakhouse—with its big oak-paneled dining room that must be a hundred years old—and asking people how they intended to escape the approaching storm. The folks I spoke to said they were all staying put. By now I was getting a little nervous—make that a *lot* nervous—and I remember feeling that what I was witnessing was similar to a scene that had played out about a century earlier on the deck of the *Titanic*.

At that point, the masses began to leave town. The talk of the wedding reception went from what a beautiful event it had been to how everybody was going to evacuate. The mood of the whole city changed in a flash. All of a sudden the always-busy French Quarter streets turned empty as the sobering news spread. And how was I feeling?

One phrase summed it up nicely: *dead in the water.* Or at least on the verge.

I knew that if Katrina hit the French Quarter directly, the whole area could be under two stories of water, and the Quarter just happened to be where my girlfriend and I were staying. We had no car and no other way out of this whole Big Easy mess.

By about 3:00 A.M., I realized that we couldn't stick around for even a moment longer. I went into total survivor mode. I like to think I'm pretty good at getting into that mode, having been on the road so much. Playing the sort of gigs I had, one gets experience in fleeing natural and man-made disasters.

I went outside on the street and ran down a cab. An actual *cab.* Can you believe there was one still available? I couldn't, and I wasn't about to let this one get away. I asked the driver, "Where are you going?" The guy said, "To the airport." I'd already heard that flights weren't getting out of there, so I told the driver, "I'll give you five hundred bucks if you take me fifty miles northwest of here." The driver just kept saying, "I *can't* do it, I *can't* do it." I told him, "You've *got* to do it." Finally, I think he just got tired of wasting time sitting there arguing with me, and eventually he said, "Okay." Once again, I'd accomplished something simply by being a persistent pain in the ass.

So I rushed off and got five hundred bucks out of an ATM—thankfully, I had that much in my account. Because it was now three in the morning, my girlfriend was half asleep, but I got her into the cab with me. I don't think she was fully aware where she was or what we were up to, but I wasn't going to leave her behind. The whole scene around us was getting crazier by the moment. Hours before, we'd been partying hard at a joyous wedding, and now here we were frantically fleeing town with hangovers.

We started to make our way through the back roads and backwaters of New Orleans, heading toward I-10 so we could eventually get to Baton Rouge. But when we hit St. Charles Avenue, we were stunned to see no cars. That was just mind-blowing. It would be like going down to Times Square and discovering there isn't a single car or person on the street.

Suddenly, this great city felt more like a scene from the Apocalypse—and it was enough to make even our driver pick up his speed a little.

In the end, we drove fifteen hours in that cab with no air-conditioning because we wanted to conserve our gas and just keep moving forward until we got as far as West Monroe. On the way there, I called Southwest on my cell phone and said, "Look, you guys canceled my flight home. What can you do for me?" The Southwest person said, "Well, we can give you a voucher for a free round trip anywhere around the country." At the time, their offer seemed pretty good, though I'd only realize later *how* good.

Even then, riding in that cab, feeling pretty mangy from the long ride, I knew I was extremely lucky to be able to get out of what would become a tragic situation for hundreds of thousands. Not everybody in the wedding party was so lucky, and some of Tracy and Brian's friends and family got trapped in New Orleans hotels for days. Tracy and Brian returned from their honeymoon having lost just about everything except each another. As I think back on it, one of the many eerie things about that experience was sensing there were only two classes of people—those who had the resources to get out of town, or at least stay put in a hotel, and those who weren't that fortunate. Nobody deserved to be left behind when the levees gave way. For me, being that close to what happened puts a very human face on the tragedy.

In the aftermath of the storm, the planned Memphis

auditions for *American Idol* were put off, for good reason. I'd previously thought vaguely about trying out for *Idol,* but now the closest spot to give it a shot was no longer a possibility. There were, however, still *Idol* auditions to come in Las Vegas. I decided, *What the hell, I've got this free plane ticket burning a hole in my pocket, and I've never been to Vegas before—so why not use the voucher and give things a go there?* Life is short, and I didn't really have that much to lose besides pocket money. The voucher represented a last chance to see if I could fit America's idea of what a good singer is—and heck, I could play a little blackjack while I was at it. Frankly, that's about as much of a thought process as went into making what would become a momentous, life-changing decision.

What can I say? Sometimes it looks bleakest right before the storm. Sometimes it looks bleakest *during* the storm. Sometimes it doesn't look bleak at all and you *still* get hammered. The point is, none of us really knows when our luck is about to change.

I was about to take a fairly long trip to lose a few bucks at blackjack, but it wouldn't matter because that little Southwest flight voucher would end up being the winning lottery ticket my dad had talked about. I just wish I had that voucher now so I could frame it forever. Perhaps the folks at Southwest can print it out for me again someday.

10
VIVA LAS VEGAS

HELL OF A DAY

I'LL BE ON MY WAY

—"Hell of a Day" by Taylor Hicks

When you think about it—and trust me, I've thought about it a lot—my father was right to liken auditioning for *American Idol* to buying a lottery ticket. There's nothing remotely realistic about trying to become a star by way of a reality show. In football terms, trying to become famous that way is like a quarterback throwing a total Hail Mary pass because he knows the clock is ticking away and he has to score *now*. At that point in my life—facing down thirty with precious little progress to show for all my time and trouble—the clock was most definitely ticking. Realistically, game time was almost up.

So was trying out for *Idol* an act of desperation?

In one sense, yes. Though trying to get on *American Idol* is a pretty wild dream in and of itself, hoping to win is a little like thinking you'll find the proverbial needle in the haystack.

Yet—and here's the other sense—the fact remains that *some-body* out there has to buy that winning lottery ticket. And though I haven't personally tested this theory yet on my own behind, I have to imagine that if you jump in enough haystacks in the course of a lifetime, you'll land on a needle eventually.

Anyway, thanks to those good folks at Southwest Airlines who sent me that glorious free travel voucher, I now didn't even have to buy a lottery ticket—or in my case, a round-trip plane ticket from Birmingham, Alabama, to Las Vegas, Nevada. All I really had to do was come up with the funds to feed and house myself for a couple of days in Las Vegas—arguably the right city for a guy like me, who'd long been bent on beating the odds.

As I boarded the plane to Vegas, I certainly wasn't thinking anything portentous—like, "This is *it*." At least, not consciously so. But an objective observer would have noted that the way things had been going for me of late, this *Idol* tryout was likely my last shot at breaking into the big time. After all, pop fame remains first and foremost a young man's—or young woman's—game, and I was getting rather long in the tooth to even be invited to play that game anymore. The official audition rules for *American Idol 5* stated that to be eligible a contestant had to be between sixteen and twenty-eight years old on August 15, 2005. I was twenty-eight years old in August, and I'd be twenty-nine in November, so my alarm clock was about to go off.

As time goes by and you continue to go through the

painful but often unavoidable process of paying your dues, waiting around for your elusive break in show business comes to seem less an act of reason and more an act of survival, perhaps even an act of faith. One lingering and lousy question never really goes away: how long can any of us afford to spend finding our way? In our quieter moments we're left to wonder: at what point does waiting around for a break become simply waiting in vain?

After my long and for the most part bumpy decade of struggling, I was beginning to feel like a rat stuck in some dark and crazy maze. All I could really think to do was keep moving in any direction where I spotted a little light. In the back of my mind, I thought of the advice friends had given to just keep going and trust in my heart that something good would come along. By now, that had pretty much become the only clear direction I had left.

And so it was really without much serious consideration of *exactly* what I was up against that I went all by myself to Las Vegas to take my chances at the *Idol* audition. I suppose I was blessed to be mostly ignorant of the whole process of how the show worked and even more ignorant of just how poorly I fit the description most would have offered of the ideal *American Idol* candidate.

In contrast to the rest of the watching world, I'd been on the road far too much in recent years to follow *American Idol* religiously. Nonetheless, I was still aware of the show's massive impact, especially since as a proud Alabaman I knew my home state had already given the show Ruben Studdard and Bo Bice.

At the very least, I figured auditioning was worth a shot, especially since I was running out of any good alternative ways to make an impression on the world. On my free flight into Las Vegas, I remember thinking about the words to "Me and Bobby McGee" and musing that Kris Kristofferson, who wrote the song, was right when he wrote, "Freedom's just another word for nothing left to lose."

Arriving in Sin City, I headed straight to my hotel—the MGM Grand Hotel and Casino, right on the Strip—and proceeded to do precisely what so many other dopey dreamers in that town had done before me: I quickly and rather expertly lost a few hundred dollars at the blackjack table. I played twenty hands and went bust on more than half of them.

If you've ever been at a blackjack table where the limits are a little too high for your tax bracket, then you know just how fast and painful things can go on the casino floor. Suffice it to say, time *really* flies when you're losing your shirt. This was a far cry from those smaller casinos I knew down on the Gulf Coast where I could quite happily bet five dollars at a time over a much more extended period. To my great displeasure, I found that losing at blackjack tables with a $20 minimum was a lot less fun than losing substantially less much closer to home.

Having run out of any spare cash to waste, I went back up to my hotel room that night feeling even more pissed off and dejected than usual. Pacing my room over and over again, I wondered what the hell I was doing here anyway. I felt like a total fool for wasting a bunch of money I didn't really have to waste. Part of me just wanted to turn around and go home before I lost anything else, including, perhaps, whatever remaining dignity I had left. After only a few short hours in the town known as Lost Wages, I was already feeling like the biggest loser around—and I'm not talking about weight loss here.

I remember looking out my hotel window that evening and doing what I'd done so often before—glumly contemplating my present and future. From my vantage point in that pricey hotel room, I could see what looked like thousands of people milling around below, all of whom appeared to be having a lot more fun than I was having. I then looked down at my depressingly thin, beat-up wallet, and wondered silently: *How many more bets on myself will I get to place?*

With nothing else to do in my near penniless state—and no one to talk to—I did the only thing I could think of doing: I nervously rehearsed for my audition over and over again. Finally, with my mind still reeling, I fell asleep sometime in the wee hours when exhaustion at long last overcame my high anxiety. My first few hours in Vegas had been anything but promising. I'd gone to bed that night—or more precisely, that morning—feeling like I was going into some sort of horrible downward spiral, as if I were about to spread my wings and then fall straight down.

Yet somehow when I woke up the next morning—
October 10, 2005, a date I'll never forget—I had a totally different and hugely more optimistic point of view. My anxiety
had suddenly and completely lifted. I don't know how to explain it, but I like to think that those three angels on my side
had somehow put me in the zone.

I'd requested a 5:00 A.M. wake-up call so I could rise before dawn and get to the auditions at the Las Vegas Convention Center as early as possible. I remember getting into a cab
as the sun was still coming up and noticing how incredibly
beautiful the brightening desert sky looked. I asked my driver,
"Does God make these sunrises every day?" The cabbie just
smiled and said, "Yes, every day."

It was a chilly desert morning, but I remember feeling
warmed by the sense that my luck was about to change. The
talk of God—and the sight of the beautiful sky overhead—
once again got me thinking about my lost friends. On some
deep, mysterious level, I felt their presence.

When I arrived at the *American Idol* auditions, I looked
around at the other people who were already lined up to take
their shot at stardom. I noticed that I didn't look like anybody
else—which was nothing new, of course. As I recall, there
were a lot of young guys trying their hardest to look a little
like Justin Timberlake or maybe Usher. Likewise, there were a
lot of young girls going for the Christina Aguilera or Beyoncé
look. Call it "fame by association." For better or worse, it
was a game I'd never win. I didn't look like *anybody* famous.

I looked significantly older and grayer than the rest of the crowd. I was also definitely the only person in sight wearing an Ashworth golf shirt. Anybody scoping out the contestants that morning probably figured I was an aging caddy trying to make a good first impression in country club hand-me-downs.

With no particular interest, one of the audition staff members handed me a number—74094, if memory serves. It wasn't exactly a number that screamed out, "I'm number one!" In a more negative mind-set, I might have turned tail right then, thinking I didn't have a chance anyway. But being so transparently different from the other younger, cooler-looking hopefuls around me made me feel better about my chances. I thought back to the lesson I'd learned as a gray-haired high schooler: standing out can end up being an advantage in the end.

For a long time I stood there waiting, lost as usual in my own head, trying to keep my focus as I prepared to take my turn. This ritual was one I'd end up repeating many times in my now unfolding *American Idol* experience. When I was competing on *Idol*, other people assumed I was being unfriendly or antisocial. But the truth of this sort of competition is that, by its nature, it's a solitary experience—at least for me it was. For all the surface camaraderie, you either *make* it on your own or *fail* on your own. When it comes down to it, you're not there to make friends, but rather to make fans.

The space where the audition took place at the Las Vegas Convention Center looked like a giant holding tent for wannabe rock and pop stars. It resembled a huge, funky convention—and like any convention, there was a certain bureaucracy that had to be dealt with. For example, before you could get to the show's producers, you had to fill out some forms and be photographed. And, of course, this being reality TV, the staff had a TV camera in your face the whole time you were there. Not that anyone was complaining. If you didn't want to be in front of a camera, you'd quite obviously come to the wrong place.

When I was asked to talk about myself, I happily told my inquisitors the truth as I saw it. "My entire life I've been a performer. Everything has been about music, about entertaining people. So that's the reason I'm here," I explained. I also danced goofily for the camera and discussed my premature gray hair and even the fact that I wasn't trying to fit in and look like anyone else—a good thing, considering my limited options in the matter.

Eventually, my time came to appear before the big producers of *American Idol,* Ken Warwick and Nigel Lythgoe. They asked me to sing for them first, so I sang my a cappella version of Sam Cooke's "A Change Is Gonna Come." After that I sang "You Are So Beautiful," co-written by Billy Preston and Bruce Fisher, but made famous by another white soul singer who moved a little funny, the great Joe Cocker.

Immediately, Ken and Nigel told me emphatically *not* to sing like Joe Cocker—they wanted me to sing like Taylor Hicks. Their comment struck a chord. This was the same conflict I'd grappled with for many years—trying to find my *own* voice to sing rather than become a carbon copy of the soulful singers I admired so much. I knew I was a good mimic, but was I a good singer?

As I chewed on that, I tried to read Nigel's and Ken's initial reactions to me for hints of what was to come. Unfortunately, they didn't exactly offer great hope that I'd succeed with the show's more famous on-camera judges, who were my next—and possibly final—stop. As I moved on to face the music one way or another, I remember Nigel saying, "You know, Taylor, they'll *never* put you through." To this day, I'm still not sure if he and Ken were trying to diminish my expectations or, rather, reduce my nerves right before my moment of truth. But, if anything, their skepticism about my making it only made me more determined to prove them wrong.

As I was leaving to face my time in the spotlight with Paula Abdul, Randy Jackson, and Simon Cowell, my potential producers gave me one last piece of advice. They told me to stand up straight and just sing my heart out. I nodded and took a deep breath.

Now more cameras were on me. As I looked over, I noticed Ken Warwick coming out of the back shadows of the room and begin rooting me on. He said, "Taylor, let it go. Let it do what it do." I took this to mean that the time had come for me to step up and really show the world what I was made of.

Of course, Simon didn't waste any time putting me on the spot. "Why are you here?" he asked with characteristic directness. "Because I want my voice heard," I told him. He immediately asked *why* I wanted my voice heard. I thought quickly and answered, "Because I've got one."

I proudly stand by those words still. My voice may not be the best or most beautiful, but it's *mine.* I continue to believe it's worth sharing. I suppose that's a problem with eventually finding your voice—after that, you tend to not shut up. At that point in the audition, though, I was just hoping I hadn't said the wrong thing.

Now came the moment of truth. As I started to sing my first song, Sam Cooke's "A Change Is Gonna Come," I remember thinking that all I really had to do was just lay it all down. For some reason, I also remember thinking that I shouldn't be too shy about using my hands as I sang. That way, they'd at least remember me.

In retrospect, it was fortunate that I sang with my eyes mostly closed. That way, I wasn't aware that Simon was looking less than impressed by what he was seeing and hearing. I believe Paula spoke first. She said she wasn't expecting what she heard and that I could "definitely" sing—which I took as a good thing. Randy said, "Dude, shake it out"—my first but hardly last "dude" from the man himself. Next, I decided to sing "Swanee River Rock" as a nod to my hero Ray Charles— the man who'd really brought me to the American soul party. From that moment on, I was *on.* Randy piped up with a somewhat surprised "Wow" and twice acknowledged that he "actually" liked me—which suggested that even *he* was taken aback by this turn of events. Randy also said he heard in my voice "a little Ray," which wasn't too hard to detect, but I still greatly appreciated being mentioned in the same breath.

Then Simon spoke and delivered one of those classic buzz-kill lines that have made him a superstar. "My problem is—and I've always said this—this not just about the voice, and you *prove* that," he told me. The far kinder, gentler, and prettier Paula took this opportunity to praise me, and Randy jumped in on my behalf too. For whatever reasons, however, Simon wouldn't be swayed. "This is a guy who should be singing background—*not* in the spotlight," he said cuttingly. Later, I'd briefly wonder if Simon was just objecting to me to be contrary, but I eventually concluded he genuinely didn't like me—at least at *first*.

Still, this was *American Idol*, after all, and in America democracy still rules. In Paula and Randy, I now had my two votes. And once those two said, "I say *yes*," it didn't really matter what the hell Simon said. For the record, I do believe his vote was, "No way in hell." Still, the bottom line was that I'd made the first cut and was now moving forward. The rarely shy Simon took his chance to share his view with everybody that they still wouldn't put me in the final group.

None of Simon's negativity really threw me, even then. At the very least I'd gotten passionate reactions—both negative and positive—and that would shape my secret strategy in the many months to come. More important, I'd finally have my chance to shine. "Sweet" is what I said when I left the room with a big smile on my face. "I'm going to Hollywood."

To the rest of the world, this was only the beginning, but for me this minor triumph meant everything. This was the break I'd been looking for. At long last, after all the missteps and disappointments, I *knew* I was finally on the right path—*my* right path. In my own mind, if nowhere else, I was no longer number 74094. In my heart and soul, I felt like number one.

From that point, my life became a wonderful, mind-blowing, and electric blur. As I recall, the *Idol* folks handed me some paperwork to fill out, but amid my euphoria the paperwork felt irrelevant. I called everyone I could think of on my cell phone to tell them the good news. Then I got on a plane and flew back home to tell everybody else.

I'm man enough to confess here and now that I cried the entire way back home. Looking back on it, I think it was a combination of relief, exhaustion, and, overwhelmingly, *happiness.* People on that plane must have thought I was crazy, but then again, people have been thinking that about me my entire life. Never before have you seen a man on a plane trip looking so ecstatic—at least not one flying coach.

I couldn't *believe* what had just happened to me. After all those years of frustration, I felt as if I'd at last caught the perfect tail wind—one that could take me exactly where I wanted to go. A lifetime of feeling judged and doubted melted away. For whatever reasons, I was more emotional on that flight than when I actually won *American Idol,* because for the first time in a very long time I felt like a winner.

Making the first cut began a very strange cycle, a crazy stop-and-start pursuit of a dream. When you watch *American Idol* on TV, after it has been expertly edited, everything seems to unfold in a flash—or, at the longest, after a short, amusing montage. The reality is quite different. Case in point: after arriving home safe from Vegas, there were two months when I was supposed to be lying low. But I wasn't very good at that, so to a large extent I kept doing what I'd been doing *before* going to the auditions. The difference was, in my little corner of the world, a certain amount of buzz collected around me. In fact, news of my making the first *Idol* cut spread like wildfire. Ever since I'd left college, I'd tried everything I could to create some buzz for myself. Now, suddenly, I couldn't stop the good buzz if I tried.

Though the *Idol* folks weren't keen on my doing gigs, I still needed to eat, I figured, and maybe even get back a few of those dollars I'd lost in Las Vegas. Music was, is, and, I'm hoping, always will be not only my life's passion but also my livelihood. And now that things were once and for all turning around for me, I couldn't see any point in stopping who I was and what I did.

When I told my father that I was going to Hollywood to be on *American Idol,* the man nearly fell on the floor. Even if I hadn't actually won the lottery quite yet, I think he was thrilled that I was still in the running. Having witnessed me struggle so much, and having worried about me for so long, my father seemed overjoyed that something was finally going my way. My whole family was almost as excited and proud as I was. They'd seen me fight so hard for any kind of exposure, and now I was going to get that exposure in the biggest, most high-profile manner. It was just a very sweet, deep feeling.

From then on, life was all one big countdown to Hollywood and the opportunities that lay in store. I could hardly wait to get to the pot at the end of the rainbow, though there'd be plenty of waiting ahead. First, I had to come out to Hollywood to be a part of the Top 45 show. If things worked out there, there'd be another month's wait before I could possibly return for the Top 24. And then there was the live-show gauntlet, and at the very top of the mountain—I hoped— *victory.*

You'd think I'd be chewing off my fingernails, calculating the long odds against ultimate success. As the time drew closer to fly out to L.A., though, I found myself getting more and more confident. On my flight out for the Top 45 show—flying coach again, for sure, but now on *American Idol*'s dime— I just remember thinking it was taking *way* too long to actually get there. It felt as if I had a very hot date with destiny, and this time I definitely didn't want to keep her waiting. My entire flight west, I sat there all wound up like a jumpy little kid on a family road trip calling out, "Are we there yet? Are we there *now?*"

At long last, we were touching down at LAX. Staring out my little window through the smoggy L.A. haze, I thought I could spot that famous Hollywood sign somewhere off in the distance. Never before in my life was I quite so ready and excited to get anywhere. This time, I thought, I wasn't just landing. This time, I'd finally arrived.

11

GONE HOLLYWOOD

OH THOSE BIG CITY NIGHTS,

IN THOSE HIGH ROLLIN' HILLS

—"Hollywood Nights" by Bob Seger

You fly into Los Angeles feeling like a star—all ready and eager for your prime-time TV close-up and that sweet major-label record deal. But then you're quickly reminded that you're only one of *dozens* of reality show hopefuls coming to town for the same selfish purpose—to get rich and famous as soon as humanly possible. It's at your hotel that you get to meet your competition face-to-face, none of whom has gray hair except you. Come to think of it, *no one* in Los Angeles has gray hair.

Right away, when I first got to Los Angeles to take part in the Top 45 show, I started sizing up the singers I was pitted against, a logical move in such charged circumstances. And it didn't take long to realize there was a lot of talent in the group. For the record, I remember being most nervous about young Paris Bennett, who I soon discovered had a wonderful voice and the personality to match. Paris' mother and grand-mother were both fine professional singers, having worked with the great group Sounds of Blackness. And Paris herself seemed to have the sort of soulful chops that could constitute trouble if I wasn't at the top of my game.

Of course, television is a visual medium, so I wasn't just *listening* to the competition but taking a close look at every-body as well. It was obvious I wasn't going to be elected king or queen of this particular prom. All around me were very attractive people like Ace Young and Katharine McPhee. If *American Idol* was going to be a beauty contest, I was twenty pounds out of luck.

But rather than feel insecure about my many flaws, I si-lenced the negative voices in my head and focused instead on what I *did* have going for me. First, there was the fact that I clearly stood out. I wouldn't get lost in the crowd.

Further, at the age of twenty-nine, I'd lived long enough to understand that most people out there are neither perfect nor perfect-looking. Presented in the right manner—with, say, some goofy charm and a sense of humor—all my flaws, physical and otherwise, could become humanizing attributes. In the end, I realized I was playing a version of *Survivor,* and the alliance I most needed to form was with the viewers at home. Paula and Randy already seemed to get me. Who knew, perhaps even Simon might get me eventually. But while I'd always listen to the judges' comments and respond to their criticism as best I could, I was well aware they weren't my ulti-mate judges.

And so from the get-go, it was the viewer at home that I was trying my best to entertain. To get their respect and sup-port, I didn't have to be the show's coolest cat—or even its flashiest. All I really had to be was somebody whom viewers could relate to and get behind when it came time to vote. Having a base of supporters as wide and active as possible would help keep me from the dreaded bottom three, or if I was lucky, bottom two.

I realized early that I had to find ways to visually stimu-late the audience. I figured chances were pretty good that plenty of people out there had crappy televisions they were watching on. And even if the picture was okay, the sound was likely to be lousy. So I thought, *This is, after all, a television show. I'd sure better find as many ways as possible to visually entertain people.* I'm a believer in looking at the bottom line, and winning a competition is ultimately one big numbers game. There's no electoral college on *American Idol*—simply the weekly will of the people.

Respecting the visual component of the competition is my explanation for the crazy dancing I did on the show, and also my purple jacket. Now, I might have done the same sort of stuff during a typical club gig, but not to the extent I did on *Idol.* In a small club I have other ways to reach out and grab an audience.

What can I say—somehow, what I showed to people viewing at home came off as appealing. Many Soul Patrol members who supported me with gusto told me they connected with this clean-cut, humble country guy who grew up in Alabama and loved football and music. Compared to the pack, I must have seemed pretty all-American—red, white, and gray, you might say.

Also, I think many woman over forty responded to me because my kind of music reminded them of music they loved when they were younger. My type of soul wasn't ultra-sexy hip-hop—it was old-school soul, and I heard from many of my older supporters that somehow I brought them back to listening to music. Nothing could make me happier.

Going into the show, I didn't really know that much about *Idol* specifically or reality TV generally. When it comes to TV viewing, I tend to tune in to sports more than anything else. But watching sports isn't such bad training for participation in a reality show. You come to understand that the viewer at home wants to *root* for a contestant. And the best way to inspire that rooting feeling is to be perceived as a guy who leaves nothing on the field, who gives everything he's got— and maybe a little more.

When it came to working a crowd onstage, I also benefited, I think, from being the only road warrior in the pack. Because I'd been at this game of trying to please a crowd much longer than most of the others, I'd gathered significantly more musical knowledge and experience to call upon. That experience came into play in a very big way when it came time to choose what songs to sing on *American Idol.*

Early in the process, I vowed to choose songs that sold my strengths, songs that were right in my sweet spot yet displayed some range, songs that—added up over the course of the season—would tell a kind of story, and in doing so, unfold my musical identity. I made my song choices in much the same way I'd come up with a set list for a show—very carefully and with an eye toward showing people who I was and where I was coming from musically.

That may explain why, when I think back on the show now, I think first and foremost not about all the perks or even the people I got to know, but of the songs that led week to week toward victory.

For Hollywood week, I sang "The First Cut Is the Deepest," a lovely song originally written by Cat Stevens back in the sixties, but later made even much more famous by Rod Stewart in the seventies and, more recently, by Sheryl Crow. With this song choice, I was trying to play to my strength as a soul singer while also trying to subtly strike a chord with as multigenerational an audience as possible. It struck me that since *American Idol* is—like nothing else on TV today—truly a show for the whole family, I'd better do my best to try and appeal to *everybody* regardless of age.

That same week I also sang Bill Withers' "Ain't No Sunshine," which just so happened to be the very same song I'd performed back in college while informally auditioning for

Passing Through. I was betting that same classic number would help me pass through to the Top 24 and the next week of *American Idol*. Looking back, I don't know if I totally nailed "The First Cut Is the Deepest," but it was still good enough to make people notice. Even if I wasn't Rod Stewart, fans said my voice had a certain appealing raspy quality. I was better on "Ain't No Sunshine," not only because I'd sung it a hundred times in clubs, but because I'd spent hours closely studying Bill Withers' stunning version from his *Live at Carnegie Hall* album, and luckily, a little of that undervalued music great's magic seemed to rub off on me.

Once I made it to the Top 24, I decided to sing Elton John's classic "Levon," which has a nice gospel feel. By this time, working with the show's musical director, Ricky Minor, and the *Idol* band, I was starting to figure out one of the keys to getting a good reaction on the show.

See, most of the classic songs that contestants sing are— in their complete form—three, four, or even five minutes long, but on *Idol* you really only have two minutes to get the job done. So, calling upon my experience leading a band, I taught myself how to get in and out of these great songs quickly while squeezing the most out of their gorgeous melodies. The idea is to make listeners feel they've heard the whole song, even though they haven't. All those years facing large crowds in bars around the South had given me valuable experience not just singing but also editing down songs and distilling their essence.

For the Top 20 show I performed "Easy," the pretty soul ballad that Lionel Richie wrote and sang during his time with the Commodores, a group that came together in my home state of Alabama. Thinking back, I'm surprised that I dared to sing such a mellow tune, rather than go out there with all guns blazing. Truthfully, I had a certain amount of confidence—earned or otherwise—that I'd be able to stick around for at least a little while, and that I should pace my selections like a set at a club—with highs and lows, quieter spots and bigger moments.

Few of my moments were bigger than the one that occurred the next week, when I was in the Top 16 and proceeded to go absolutely nuts singing "Takin' It to the Streets," one of Michael McDonald's first great songs with the Doobie Brothers. Intuitively, I sensed the time had come to bust out a tune that would allow me to strut my stuff and knock everybody's socks off. And my rendition appeared to do exactly that.

By now, we were down to the Top 12 finalists, which meant it was time for the surviving singers to move out of our hotel and settle into Los Angeles as if it were home—though, of course, it was a home where we could never get too comfortable.

Once upon a time—during the show's first three seasons—the *American Idol* contestants all lived together in a mansion in the hills of Bel Air. But by the time I arrived for Season 5, we were reduced to living in very nice but not exactly lavish *American Idol* "dorms." We resided in a big apartment complex with four guys to an apartment—at least, until some of us started to get bounced from the show, and thus, the lodgings too. I lived with Elliott Yamin, Ace Young, and Chris Daughtry. Elliott and I shared one bedroom, Ace and Chris the other. As you might imagine, it could get awkward living with the same people you were competing against. My own way of coping was to keep my eyes on the prize, which meant keeping to myself as much as possible. If you asked my roommates, they'd tell you there were times when I was fun—but other times when I was a monster. And they'd be right. Then again, I was straight up with everyone—I really was there looking for *fans,* not friends.

So what is it really like being a contestant on *American Idol?*

It's the question I get asked perhaps more than any other, and typically I respond with a quick, "It was cool." I'd now like to take this opportunity to elaborate. Being on *American Idol* is wonderfully exciting and terribly exhausting, but not always in that order. It's the best of times and the worst of times. It's also a whole lot of work, and you don't really know how the job is going to pay until it's over. That said, *American Idol* is one of the most notable cultural phenomena of our lifetimes for a good reason. It's made television history by establishing itself as a unique place where dreams like mine actually do come true.

Reflecting on it, I believe the *Idol* experience was signifi-

cantly different for me than it was for many of the other contestants. After all, many of my competitors were much younger
and less set in their ways. I'd gotten used to almost total freedom living on the road, and freedom was simply one of those
things the *American Idol* machine couldn't afford to give you.
On a show like *Friends,* the actors were the stars and were
paid accordingly. On *American Idol,* the biggest star is always
going to be the show itself. The show is one of the world's
most valuable and powerful brands, and the producers pro-
tect it zealously.

American Idol is also a live program that has to get on the
air twice or sometimes three times a week, and thus adherence
to the schedule is paramount—for crew, judges, and contestants. As a result, my fellow contestants and I lived inside a
strange traveling compound, with almost every minute of
every waking hour controlled to a remarkable degree. I thoroughly understand why Team *Idol* is so protective. On the
other hand, I'm quite confident there are juries on big mur-
der cases that are far less sequestered, and I imagine there are
attractive young virgins who are less doggedly chaperoned.

If you're lucky enough to find yourself on the show
someday, you'll soon discover that you live at the beck and
call of the producers who make the show happen. To put on a
live show that often is more than a full-time job for just about
everybody involved. As a finalist, you're always either picking
songs, learning songs, rehearsing songs, or doing press and pro-
motion in the form of an endless procession of photo shoots,

interviews, and anything that can forward the greater good of *Idol.* Even Sunday, my traditional day of rest, was now a busy one because that's when the show's cast shot the Ford commercials. Throughout it all, there's a tremendous amount of time to hurry up and wait, but very little free time. Ultimately, such a crazy schedule keeps you not just busy but humble, and I think the producers like it that way.

So yes, I owe *American Idol* a lot, but just to keep things totally real, I want you to rest assured that *American Idol* does an excellent job of finding ways for someone like me to help repay that debt. Many people I meet are under the impression a person becomes rich and famous just by *getting on* a reality show. Nothing could be further from the truth. Reality TV is, among other things, a very cost-effective form of broadcasting. Instead of paying actors millions to star in a show, a producer can instead pay contestants something closer to room and board and then take a piece of the action they bring in.

When you first latch on to a reality show opportunity, the last thing you want to do is piss off the producers of the very same show you're now trying to win. But in the case of *Idol* and me, my age, experience, and rabble-rousing instincts pushed me close to the edge. The fact is, I noted the way the pie was being carved up and tried to get the Top 24 contestants and their families together to discuss this situation. Once we'd gathered in a room, I said, "If we all get together and organize, they'll *have* to negotiate with us because right now they don't have a show without us."

Yes, I'm the man who tried to organize the Top 24 of *American Idol*, and let the record show I failed miserably. Most people said this was the best position they'd ever been in, so why not sign the contract? There's some logic to that point of view. But my point here is people should go into these shows with their eyes wide open. And the sometimes harsh truth is that on these reality shows you're at the mercy of a system that's very cozy. Sometimes, it feels like everybody is getting rich *except* you.

One of the few times people on the show really kicked back was at our great Wednesday night dinners. These were in essence "last suppers" with whoever got kicked off on the results show. They were important opportunities not just to say goodbye to the departed but also for the remaining contestants to blow off steam, see some family, and just recharge their batteries so they could dive into the next week. Other than on Wednesday nights, the contestants were very tied together—sort of like prisoners on an especially glitzy chain gang.

While you're on the show, you're not getting rich. Your basic needs are met. You're also given a cell phone and a small clothing budget. You're discouraged from living on the Internet or doing pretty much anything else that might take you outside the busy world of *American Idol*. The show's producers try in every way to keep you out of trouble—both for your good and theirs. Of course, there are times when contestants, being human, buckle under the pressure.

I fondly remember one night when Elliott and I attended

a Lakers game and, reacting to all the pressure, I probably had ten beers. After that, I just remember the two of us rolling around having a ball. I really needed an occasional moment like that to get out of my own head because it could feel like we were playing a Super Bowl every week.

Then there was the time that Elliott, Bucky Covington, and I went to Las Vegas overnight to do something with Barry Manilow. Perhaps sensing danger, the show's producers told us we couldn't go out. Now, you might be able to convince a sixteen-year-old he was grounded in Vegas, but not this twenty-nine-year-old. So what did I do? I corrupted Elliott and Bucky, of course, and the three of us snuck out of our hotel and basically hit every red carpet that was happening in Las Vegas that night. We almost got away with our great escape too—except some pictures showed up. Thanks to some fans with camera phones, our perfect crime in Vegas was compromised.

These were simply a few mad chases for a freedom that most of the time was unobtainable. By and large, we did what we were told, living less like rock stars and more like astronauts kept in isolation. Looking back, I understand why we all lived as we did. As an *American Idol* contestant, we needed to be entirely focused on the show. The producers had a vested interest in encouraging single-mindedness, but it made sense for the contestants too.

♫

Having made it into the Top 12, I knew there'd be more and more people tuning in to the show to see all the action, so I couldn't afford to lose any momentum now. On the March 14, 2006, show—a Stevie Wonder theme night—I sang "Living for the City," one of Stevie's strongest and most socially conscious songs. As if singing that great song weren't enough, I also took the opportunity to try out a few funky Sly and the Family Stone moves as well. I think everybody enjoys seeing a crazy white dude take his chances getting funky, and, if I do say so myself, I was pretty fly for a white guy that week.

The next week *American Idol* had a fifties musical theme, and I tried to once again hit a few generations at once by performing "Not Fade Away," which Buddy Holly first recorded, before it was recorded by the Rolling Stones and the Grateful Dead, among many others. I tried my best to infuse a little of the Dead's version right in the middle of my tribute to Buddy. I don't think it was necessarily my best performance, but it was strong enough to keep my quest alive.

Having covered the fifties, the remaining Top 10 finalists moved on to the music of the twenty-first century for the March 28 show. This theme allowed me to show a different and decidedly more modern side of myself by singing "Trouble" by Ray LaMontagne, a great new singer-songwriter whose work you'd probably never expect to hear played anywhere near *American Idol*. As such things go, it was a fairly gutsy selection to make, and one I'm proud of still.

Sadly, the same can't be said of my choice for the April 4

country-music-themed show—John Denver's "Take Me Home Country Roads." I remember calling my friend Keb' Mo' that week, and his telling me *not* to sing that song—that it was a fine song but just totally wrong for me. I thought it was too late to switch my song by then, and that it would be a nice number to sing for the people of West Virginia. The result was my weakest moment on the show thus far. I should have listened to Kevin and taken some other country road that week. I was fortunate that I performed first that week and somehow lived to sing another day.

I suppose everybody can have an off week, but on *American Idol,* you sure as hell mustn't have two in a row. Happily, the next week's Queen show was one of my favorites of the year. I picked "Crazy Little Thing Called Love" to sing, and I went suitably crazy. I think I may have been channeling the late great Queen front man Freddie Mercury that night. The surviving members of the band seemed to dig my act, even my increasingly famous—or is that *infamous?*—dance moves.

The next week we were down to just seven people, and I gave what I would personally rank as my best performance of the season. I will never sing "You Send Me" anywhere as well as Sam Cooke, but that night was probably as close as this white boy will ever get.

The April 25 show—with its theme of classic love songs— would prove an especially difficult and controversial week for me. The producers somehow concluded that I couldn't per- form my first choice—"Try a Little Tenderness" as my salute to Otis Redding—because in their view it wasn't really a classic love song. Their decision baffled me then, and frankly it still does now, but I had no choice but to switch songs at the last minute. So instead I sang "Just Once," a romantic smash for James Ingram, who sweetly told me that I pulled off the song in the end. I suppose I'll have to take his good word for it, and again I lived to sing another day.

For the May 2 show, we were down to only five contestants, and that meant I got to pick two songs. First I had to choose a song from the year of my birth, so I sang a 1976 smash that defined exactly what I was doing on the show—"Play That Funky Music." My most vivid memory of that performance is of me falling down on the floor and Ryan Seacrest falling on the floor with me. Where else in prime time are you going to see a white boy from Alabama and a white boy from Georgia getting down like that?

For my other song, I had to pick something from the current *Billboard* charts. Thinking fast, I asked to sing George Harrison's "Something" from the Beatles' recent collection of number one hits, which fortunately was still on the charts back then. That thought—along with the hard work of our music clearance person—allowed me to sneak a genuine Fab Four classic onto our show when everyone else was busy singing contemporary material that was almost certainly less familiar and less distinctive to many of our viewers. For accessibility and quality, it remains impossible to beat the Beatles.

Now there were just four of us left in the competition—

myself, Katharine McPhee, Elliott Yamin, and Chris Daughtry. This was another crucial, do-or-die moment for all of us, and to get any further we'd have to reckon with the King himself. For the Elvis theme show, I picked two songs that showed some range: the endlessly cool "Jailhouse Rock" and the deeply moving "In the Ghetto." I couldn't sing them quite like the King did, but I did my best. As always, Ricky Minor and the band really helped me shine.

After Chris Daughtry was eliminated—to the surprise of many—we were down to our final three, and an opportunity arose to really take in exactly what was happening to me. *American Idol* followed me home to Birmingham, where I received a homecoming party I'll never forget.

Believe it or not, Alabama governor Bob Riley named May 12, 2006, Taylor Hicks Day. They even gave me the key to the city. To go from local underachiever to local and even state hero in just a few short months was a pretty surreal—and yet entirely satisfying—experience. I'll never forget the experience of riding in the back of a stretch limousine with fifteen state troopers heading down the Interstate. There I was, an overnight sensation traveling down some of the same roads I'd driven while going to and from gigs, back then hoping that I wouldn't get stopped by a state trooper because I couldn't afford any speeding tickets. I always thought you had to be the president—or at least Coach Bear Bryant—to get that kind of deluxe treatment.

It's funny how when your dream comes true, it tends to be different from what you imagined—sometimes it's even bigger in scope. My dream was always to be able to make a good living singing and maybe have a decent-sized audience waiting for me in venues when I got there. But coming home to Birmingham as an *Idol* finalist and being given a hero's welcome, I realized something much more grand and unlikely was happening. I'd wished for steady work, and somehow I'd stepped into a full-blown pop culture phenomenon. In the early days of my *Idol* climb especially, there'd been no time to stop and mentally process what was going on. But that homecoming gave me a chance to take stock. It made me pause for some badly needed deep breaths, laugh, and just be thankful.

On May 15, with my future record company boss, Clive Davis, advising the contestants, I sang Bruce Springsteen's great song "Dancing in the Dark," one of the most compelling songs ever written about being frustrated. Probably it didn't hurt that I was really *feeling* that song that night. I don't think I'd even kissed a girl for almost a year, so I connected easily with the desperation and the loneliness in the song's lyrics. Interestingly, I almost didn't get to sing this song, since Chris Daughtry had already picked it for himself. But when Chris went home, the song was mine to use.

That same night, I got to sing "You Are So Beautiful," written by Billy Preston and Bruce Fisher, but based on the famous spare arrangement by the great Joe Cocker. Back in Las

Vegas, I'd been warned to be myself, not a clone of Joe Cocker. Now I got to pay tribute to one of my soul influences and be myself doing it. I also finally got to sing Otis Redding's "Try a Little Tenderness," and yes, to me it was still one classic love song. As it turned out, I was glad the producers had made me wait for a truly dramatic moment to sing that song—the same song that had so affected me back in the fourth grade.

On May 22, I sang my last time for America's vote, and I revisited two of my better moments from the show—performing "Living for the City" and "Levon" one more time. For "Living for the City," I debuted my famous purple jacket. It was something I'd spotted in a store weeks earlier. I knew that if I made the finale, I wanted to wear it—one way or another I'd definitely go out in high style. I also debuted "Do I Make You Proud?"—a song that was originally meant for my pal Elliott to sing. Since Elliott had been eliminated, the song was given to me after I butted heads with the producers over the original song I was given. In the end, the song seemed to go over pretty well.

By the time the show ended, I felt as if I'd found the perfect groove, that at long last my instincts were functioning flawlessly, helping me make all the right decisions in regard to song choices, delivery, and presentation. I was comfortable with the show, with the theater, with the audience live and at home. I even felt comfortable with myself. Either way—win or lose—I felt like a winner, and that was good enough.

And when I actually *won* the title on that unforgettable night, I was more than ready to celebrate. Not long after the final credits rolled, I ran over to Ryan Seacrest's table ready to drink a whole bottle of bubbly, but I believe there was only one glass left at that point. That was probably for the best, since in the next forty-eight hours, my first as an *Idol,* I'd get about two hours of sleep. Like that champagne, victory was sweet, but my work was far from over.

As I said at this book's beginning, deep down I felt I was going to win *American Idol.* Truth be told, I had a *very* unofficial and ethically questionable focus group that assured me I was making a connection with the people who were out there watching.

See, when you sign up for *American Idol,* you're supposed to stop selling any independent records you may have made up to that point. But for two very good reasons— namely, money and survival—I might have absentmindedly allowed some friends of mine to keep selling my music out of one little local store in Birmingham, Alabama. Being famous and still cash-poor can be frustrating, so you do what you have to do.

The truth is, my already shaky personal finances took a hit while I was trying to win the show. In the year or so before going on *Idol,* I was just starting to sell lots of T-shirts, hats, and CDs. The band merchandise brought in a pretty penny—even a few pretty pennies. Then that revenue disappeared. Once I was one of the last two finalists on *Idol*, though, I knew something was happening when I heard one little store in my hometown was selling tons of CDs. That money allowed me to buy that famous purple jacket. Apparently, sometimes a little crime *does* pay.

If I could go back in time, would I do anything differently when it came to competing on *American Idol*? Absolutely not—except possibly I'd try and lose twenty pounds *before* I was on the show and not immediately after. I appreciate that *American Idol* did things for me that nothing else could have—or would have. I thank everyone there for using their talents to help further my career as well as theirs.

As a veteran Idol, I hold this truth to be self-evident: I owe *American Idol* a huge debt. In a million ways, the show changed my life for the better. *Idol* gave me my chance to present what I had to offer to the world. It gave me the break I'd spent a decade desperately searching for. Somehow, in just a matter of weeks, seemingly everybody in America knew my name, face, and hair. I captured the biggest platform imaginable to launch my career on a national—and I hope international—level.

But beyond making me famous, the show offered countless experiences that would otherwise be unimaginable for a guy like me. Where else on earth was I going to have Stevie Wonder tell me I had soul (he should know) . . . or have Barry

Manilow say he liked my "whiskey tenor" (turns out all those whiskeys I drank paid off) . . . or have Andrea Bocelli offer his professional opinion that I possess an extraordinary voice (it's sort of like Ted Williams saying, "You can really hit, kid.")?

And lest we forget, without *American Idol* what would have been the odds of Rebecca Romijn pleading with me to sing "Heartbreak Hotel" to her? One in a billion? One in a trillion? I don't think they've yet built a computer that can calculate the real number.

Beyond the power to make dreams come true, *Idol* offers something that, when I'm thinking about it objectively, I can see is even more important. It brings people of all ages together in a way too few things do today. It calls individual family members from their separate nooks inside the home and has them gather—and laugh, hoot, and holler—in a central location. At work, it coaxes people out of their cubicles and into the hall to debate the latest results. I don't know if *American Idol* is a superior replacement to the family television I grew up on, like *The Cosby Show* or *Mama's Place,* but it's the best we've got, folks.

Finally, what other TV show is able to introduce millions of young people to the eternal beauty of "You Send Me" by Sam Cooke? To me, that alone represents a valuable public service.

In the end all I ever tried to do was entertain people—that's what I did in the clubs, and that's what I did in those first months of 2006 for the millions who didn't want to leave the comfort of their living rooms. When you're an entertainer, it's your great privilege to touch people's lives in a distant and yet seemingly personal way. *American Idol* gave me the chance to do that on a level that is truly breathtaking. For that and so many other things, I'll never forget the show or its unique and strange place in my life.

12

TAKIN' IT TO
THE STREETS

TAKE THIS MESSAGE TO MY BROTHER

YOU WILL FIND HIM EVERYWHERE.

—"Takin' It to the Streets" by Michael McDonald

B efore we go any further, I'd like to share what I believe is an important and, I hope, extremely helpful fitness tip: If you ever *really* want to lose weight in a hurry, all you have to do is become a contestant on *American Idol.* Next, do whatever is necessary to get past all of Simon Cowell's pot-shots and find some way to actually win the competition. With that accomplished, you merely have to wait for the pounds to start dropping. I call this the *American Idol* Victory Lap Diet. The secret of this comprehensive weight loss program is that when you win *American Idol,* you become so incredibly active—so around-the-clock busy—that you swap eating for sprinting.

After taking that quick celebratory sip of champagne backstage right after winning the *American Idol* title, the next few largely sleepless days and nights became a blur of nonstop activity. In America everybody loves a winner—or at least wants to interview one—so I found myself running the media gauntlet until I dropped. As I recall, there was little time to stop and think, and even less time to eat. Suddenly, it was as if the whole world were conspiring to keep me constantly moving and thus always burning calories. My entire lifestyle changed radically, and my body changed with it. Over the next month or two I lost something like twenty-five pounds, so even as I felt the love of the American people, there was significantly less of me to love. Lest you think I turned into a hardbody, though, I must confess that I still have a little of that belly that probably earned me a few sympathy votes. And somehow my *Idol* weight loss still doesn't look nearly as good on me as it does on, say, Carrie Underwood.

Question: So how do you go from being completely unknown to completely overexposed in a matter of weeks?

Answer: You just do exactly what I did.

By the time of the *American Idol* finale, my face was everywhere. Sure, so too was Katharine McPhee's, but let's be honest: Katharine's face is a lot easier on the eyes than mine. When you reach the level of total media saturation I did in May 2006, logic and good taste would suggest that the time had come to step back for a moment, lie a little lower, and perhaps even allow the American public to miss you for a day or two.

However, almost immediately after winning the show, I was approached by Simon Fuller—the original creator of *Idol*—who made me an offer I felt I couldn't refuse, especially considering the financial shape I was in. Yes, greed claimed my soul, and instead of stepping away from the spotlight a little, I agreed to step forward a little more. Instead of just being on the air a couple of times a week, I began popping up on every channel, dancing around and trying to sell viewers a Ford truck. In the spots, I sang a song in which I dared to ask the world, "Are you ready for me?" *Ready* for me? Chances are, by that time you were getting pretty damn *sick* of me. Hell, *I* was getting sick of me—and that was a problem because I *am* me.

It's hard for people to look forward to seeing you again if you never bother to leave their sight. Those Ford commercials gave people a chance to get tired of me. Striking while the irons are hot makes a lot of sense in terms of dollars and cents, but it's also an excellent way to get overexposed. And I didn't want my career run like that. I was looking to win a marathon, not just a sprint or two.

Listen, I can hear some of you out there thinking, *Shut up, Taylor, and be thankful that the show made you famous.* And truly, I am. But I sure as hell didn't set out to become famous as a car salesman, and somewhere about the time I spotted the hundredth airing of that commercial I realized my priority had to be building a life in music for the long term.

Reality TV has brought Andy Warhol's idea of everybody

being famous for fifteen minutes much closer to being, well, a reality. But my music is not some fad to me—this is my *life,* and I wanted to work with people who were more interested in the long view than the quick hit.

Based on my admittedly limited experience, being a celebrity can be a bit like being in a romantic relationship with millions of people at the same time—and just about as exciting and exhausting. Just as with any personal relationship, you realize that familiarity can breed a little contempt. As a result, sometimes it's a really good idea to make yourself scarce for a while. An old song I heard once put this idea perfectly: "How Can I Miss You When You Won't Go Away?"

However, for me lying low was simply not in the cards. As soon as I won the *American Idol* title, all sorts of crazy offers started pouring in. I was being sent screenplays for films to star in, including at least one movie about *me.* I don't believe anyone pitched a romantic beach movie titled *From Katharine to Taylor*—the equivalent of what Justin Guarini did with Kelly Clarkson in *From Justin to Kelly*—but then again I might have missed such an offer amid all the chaos.

Right after I won *American Idol*—on the same surreal day my *People* magazine cover story came out—I was in Los Angeles when I got a phone call out of the blue from a man named Tony Gumina. Tony explained that he was the president of the Ray Charles Marketing Group, and he asked if I had a few hours to spare. For anybody who had anything to do with Ray Charles, I could find the time. Tony said he was going to come pick me up. He didn't exactly tell me what he was picking me up for or where the hell I was going, but in this case I was digging the mystery.

Just a little while later, I was picked up in Ray Charles' old Mercedes. Now, I'm getting harder to impress these days, but as I dropped into the backseat of my hero's car, I did say, "*Damn,* this is cool." Then I was told I was going to Ray's office and his studio. Now I was getting really excited.

I'd just come back from the beach the day before, so I happened to have a really bad sunburn. My arms were peeling terribly, so as I made my entrance to Ray's place, I was standing there scratching myself like crazy. When they saw me, the ladies in Ray's office flipped out. I guess in some small way my presence reminded them of Ray. One lady kept saying over and over, "I *told* you. I *told* you it was in him. I told you he has a little Ray in him." She insisted that what I was doing was helping reinvent soul music and that Ray would have really dug me because he was the original inventor, having taken R&B and gospel and melded them into soul music. For me, there could be no higher compliment.

They gave me the private tour of Ray's old stomping grounds. They told me about a trapdoor and the place where Ray had kept all his tapes. Having studied Ray's music for most of my life, I told them that I was most interested in some particular live cuts of Ray in Tokyo, Japan, because I'd heard some cuts from Tokyo that were absolutely incredible.

We went into Ray Charles' vaults, where everything is written in Braille. They explained to me that Ray was the one who knew every inch of the place—and he'd done it by humming bars of music. For instance, he knew which door would take a four-bar measure for him to reach from a certain point. The man must have had perfect time, because in his own place he knew exactly where he was at all times. My respect for the man was only growing. So there I was standing in my hero's vault, surrounded by some of the greatest music ever made. I bent down and picked up a random box of tapes, and it turned out to be exactly what I was looking for—Ray live in Tokyo.

The folks there asked me if I wanted to become the first outside artist to record in Ray's old studio. Immediately, I said that I'd be honored to record where my hero did, and I *will*. I hope the next record I make will be at Ray's place.

Then they took me to Ray's wardrobe closet, and there were Ray's classic jackets hanging right there. They told me I should try one on. Since they suggested it, I did exactly that. And wouldn't you know it, Ray's old jacket fit just like a glove—as if it had been personally tailored for me right down to the sleeves. They told me that when I come back, I can take that jacket home.

Listen, I know I'm nowhere near the man Brother Ray

was, and I never will be. No one will ever touch his genius or his legacy. But no matter what happens to me over the years, that jacket is one soulful hand-me-down I'll treasure the rest of my life.

I could hardly wait to start recording my first big album, but I'd *have* to wait because I still had one outstanding obligation to the *Idol* folks, and that was being the headlining act along with the rest of the Top 10 finalists on the *American Idol* tour—officially known as *Pop-Tarts Presents American Idols Live*.

In some ways, this tour was a dream—and not just because we got all the Pop-Tarts we could eat, free. Instead of living the performing life in baggage class, I got to spend my summer vacation on a big tour bus, traveling from city to city, not having to figure out how to pay for my hotel rooms. As for the *mood* on the bus, let's just say it was interesting, with everybody getting caught up in their own careers, working on their own management and record deals, and trying to ensure they'd have a career going when the tour ended. The truth is, there were times when we got on each other's nerves. The saving grace, though, was that now when we got on each other's nerves, we all had our own hotel rooms to hide out in for a while.

Then there was the matter of the audience. On the *Idol* tour, I found myself playing to crowds that were much bigger than I'd ever imagined. The tour production people and the musicians were all great and professional. And based on the squeals of delight from fans around the country, the people who came to see us had a great time listening to all their *Idol* favorites.

Yet performing as the final, headlining act on this massive and massively successful tour was still a learning experience. Here's one big thing I learned: I was *not* born to play arenas. Everything I've learned about music is about making a *connection,* and at least for me, a giant arena is not the best place to make a connection. Getting to play all those little joints along the way and really look my audiences in the eye has spoiled me forever. Performing is a relationship between you and your audience, and in that relationship less can definitely be more. Singing in an arena, it takes much longer to feel the energy of the crowd and feed off that energy. That shared energy is what I hunger for—more than money and more than fame. So if I had my dream in all its fine-tuned glory, it would be to play great theaters and clubs for the rest of my life.

On the *Idol* tour, I tried to bring something new, something old, and something blues to the festivities. I thought everyone would comment—you know, say something like, "Wow, Taylor's playing guitar, he's playing harmonica." But that's not the sort of thing most people notice in an arena. I believe I'm the first American Idol ever to play a solo on any instrument, and you'd think one critic covering the tour would have commented on that. But I guess those critics were so whipped after watching nine other acts first, they just didn't notice.

Being the final act on the *American Idol* tour had a strange tension to it that I was not used to. See, when you're playing clubs, you can assume that if people are there at midnight, they probably don't mind being there at 1:00 A.M. too. Hell, they may even stick around longer in hopes of *not* going home alone—or maybe going to some other home they might like better.

The *Idol* tour was something else entirely. It was more like playing the family version of *Beat the Clock*. You could look out into the audience and see parents eyeballing their watches, thinking, *I've got to get these kids home to bed.* Of course, the people in nightclubs think about getting people to bed, but in a *whole* different way.

So, coming on around ten o'clock, I sometimes thought I should just sing "Takin' It to the Streets" and get the heck off—because Junior's got a math test in the morning and Mom's getting worried about being late for her car pool. That's about as un-rock-and-roll a thought as you can possibly have.

On the other hand, I genuinely loved that, for a lot of kids in the audience, this was their first concert ever. It took me back to my own first big concert, when I got to see Tina Turner and Lionel Richie on the same bill in Birmingham. I know I'll never forget that night.

Here's another funny thing about the *Idol* tour that didn't seem all that funny at the time: generally, when you play a big show, you know you're playing to your fans—or at least to people who like you a little. On the *Idol* tour, though, you were reminded very bluntly that you might not be *everybody's* cup of tea. Never before in my career had I started to sing to somebody in the front row only to realize they were holding up a sign reading, "I Voted for Chris!"

Just to make things a little more complicated—and to keep things real for myself musically—I took part in a separate shadow club tour with my old road band, now known as the Little Memphis Blues Orchestra. The way it worked is that the band booked a separate tour playing cool clubs around the country on many of the same nights the *Idol* tour was in town. Since the *Idol* show was over relatively early— hey, we were a family show—I could usually hook up with the guys and do a set as a special, semi-surprise guest in the midnight hour. And even if I couldn't get there in time, people would still get a chance to see the Little Memphis Blues Orchestra guys in their own right. Trust me, those guys didn't need me to show up as much as I might like to think.

Now, you might assume that trying to do two tours at once would quickly create burnout. Instead, getting the chance to sing some of my old songs and other cool covers kept me sane—or at least saner—in the midst of the insanity of the *Idol* tour, which at times felt more like playing a theme park than a nightclub. Sitting in with the guys again put me right back in my element—playing with my band of brothers, making the music we all loved for a bunch of people who loved it right back.

Those brief, after-hours reunions really helped. I hope they also helped the guys. One of the tough things about being based in a place like Birmingham is that it can be extremely difficult to get people from big labels and big management companies to check out what you're doing. So it made me very happy to see the guys playing lots of ultra-cool places like the Viper Room on the Sunset Strip and more than holding their own with the cool crowd from the coast. Let's face it, how many honky-tonk redneck soul bands ever get to play on the Sunset Strip?

When your dreams come true, it only makes sense to bring the people who helped get you there along for the ride. First, it's the right thing to do. And second, it keeps you rooted in the things that matter—the things that made you who you are in the first place. Playing those second shows late at night while on the *Idol* tour was a way of staying connected with my roots and my true musical self. And as I've said, I looked forward to every one of those after-hours gigs because I felt revived afterward. I felt like I was coming home

There was one extra-special stop on the big *American Idol* tour that I'll never forget, and that was our trip to the White House. In the middle of takin' it to the streets *Idol*-style, we found time to squeeze in a side trip to 1600 Pennsylvania

Avenue. In a funny way, this too ended up becoming a kind of homecoming.

First, I should tell you a little about my own less than impressive political history and brush with the bitter world of electoral politics. Let the record show that the voting hasn't *always* gone my way. Back in sixth grade, I ran for class president and lost. At least, that's what the official vote tally indicated. I've always wondered if possibly I was considered too much of a hell-raiser back then to be handed higher office, and perhaps the teachers decided to pick the president themselves that year. Since the election results weren't reviewed by the Supreme Court, I suppose we'll never really know.

My official Taylor Hicks for Sixth-Grade Class President campaign slogan back then was one I still live by: "I can do my best, and do no more." As it turned out, those words—and that attitude—may not have gotten me elected class president, but they *did* help bring me eventually to the White House.

Putting all politics aside, I was on cloud nine as I walked into the White House to meet the president of the United States. Even after experiencing all the glitz of Hollywood, walking through the entrance of that famous house took my breath away. And what made it cooler was that I was about to meet a friend there. As fate would have it, my ninth-grade English teacher from Hoover High School, Susan Dryden—these days known as Susan Whitson—was now working as First Lady Laura Bush's press secretary. Having my former teacher there—who'd taken an interest in me back when I was a troubled teen—not only made this big moment more special, it also made it possible.

Being the kind of shameless working musician I am, I'm forever putting my music in the hands of people I know, especially anyone who might help me get my music out there to a broader audience. I'd kept up with my former teacher's progress over the years as she rose through the ranks of government jobs. I'd even sent her one of my first CDs years ago, hoping that perhaps she could help me score a gig playing on Capitol Hill. I figured she was someone special, someone who was really going to accomplish important things, so I wanted her to know what I was doing.

Anyway, the day after Christmas in 2005, while passing through the first stages of *American Idol,* I was reading the *Birmingham News*—I've always been a pretty religious daily newspaper reader—when I discovered that Ms. Whitson was now serving in the White House. I immediately decided to give her a call. She took the time to send me back a nice e-mail. Then when *American Idol* started taking off for me, Ms. Whitson and I began e-mailing each other little updates. It was really nice to know she was still on my side.

You can see where I'm going with this. When it came time to head out on the *American Idol* tour—including a date in the Washington, D.C., area—I wrote suggesting that maybe I could stop by and meet the president. Hey, it never hurts to ask. After that, one thing led to another, and a time was arranged for America's biggest show to visit the ultimate American venue. This was my kind of Hoover High School reunion.

When I'd won *American Idol* in May, a lot of people had made note of the fact that I'd received more votes than the president had received in the previous election: sixty-three million for me and fifty-nine million for him, but hey, who's counting? To be fair, people were allowed to vote for me more than once, whereas I do believe that at presidential polling places repeat customers are frowned upon.

Anyway, since this issue of similar vote totals has come up, let me be the first to say that it's clear to me which one of us has the more important job. I like to think I'm a decent campaigner, though. I feel as if I've been campaigning for my music for years—only instead of shaking hands and kissing babies, I've been shaking hands and singing soul songs.

The day we went to the White House, you could feel the tension in the air because of the ongoing conflict in the Middle East. The president and British prime minister Tony Blair were holding a huge joint press conference that day, so a visit from the *American Idol* gang during a time of heightened alert took a backseat, as well it should have.

But at last the moment arrived. I walked into the Oval Office first, and there he was—the leader of the free world taking time out of his day to meet the *American Idol* contingent. To me, President Bush comes across as a regular guy—although one with the weight of the world resting on his shoulders. Considering how complicated our world has gotten today, anybody who wants to take on that particular gig is A-OK in my book—and this *is* my book.

President Bush gave us all a little tour of the Oval Office and posed for a group photo with the whole gang. Then he took an individual photo with each of us. In return, we gave him a harmonica engraved with the words "American Idol 2006." I also personally presented him with a black "Soul Patrol" T-shirt. Yes, even in the Oval Office, even during a time of war, I was bold enough to work the room a little. President Bush spoke to us all about sticking to our beliefs and holding on to those beliefs even as our celebrity grew. I appreciated those words, as well as the idea that our celebrity was still growing.

Then the White House staff let the photographers into the room to take their pictures, and I swear it was like they'd let the piranhas out of their holding tank. Even the president has his presidential paparazzi. At least in that way, show business and politics seem not so different after all.

Time magazine reported that I actually had another prominent fan in the White House: Secretary of State Condoleezza Rice, who was born and raised in Birmingham, Alabama. The magazine noted that Secretary Rice took time out of her diplomatic duties to await the results of *American Idol*. I thought that sort of dedication was very nice, and maybe just a little scary. Of course, I took time to read about what Ms. Rice and the president were doing every day, so in some ways it was only fair.

It's unfortunate I didn't get a chance to meet Secretary Rice when I stopped by the Oval Office that day. With both of us being Alabamians, perhaps our paths will yet cross.

In the end, my other lasting and fond memory of that amazing trip to the White House is of the few minutes I was privileged to spend with some very soulful members of the White House kitchen staff who took the time to rush right over to me and shake my hand. One of the White House cooks told me I ought to sing more Ray Charles songs. Now that, my fellow Americans, is the kind of executive order I can really get behind.

The *American Idol* tour ended in the fall of 2006 on an appropriately silly high note with our excellent tour crew launching an effective surprise Silly String attack on all of the tour performers—a truly colorful ending to our great adventure.

When you find yourself thrust together with all sorts of people in these strange show-business situations, it's an interesting and surprisingly intimate experience. Show business tends to draw in a lot of folks who are looking for love. Why else would it be so important to us to have strangers stand up and applaud when we enter the room?

When you're in the show-business bunker with other folks, there are times when you make fast and furious friends—friends who can last a lifetime. For instance, I hope that Elliott and I will stay in touch for many years to come. There are also times when it feels as though you've got a whole new family of annoying in-laws you don't necessarily want around all the time. Yet just like in real life, sometimes you've got no other choice.

On our *Idol* tour, conversations did get testy every once and a while, and there were times when things would get tense with some of the other contestants, but most of the time it was all pretty cordial. Despite our many differences, the other contestants and I still shared an experience that gave us one hell of a unique bond. In retrospect, I realize our tour was a necessary way for everybody involved to grow up and grow away from one another as we moved on to the next step. As we said our goodbyes, I wished everybody good luck—some a little more good luck than others.

After the *Idol* tour ended I felt exhausted, so I took a couple of days of vacation before beginning the exciting task of making my first major-label album. Though I'd spent many years traveling in a broken-down van, I wasn't terribly comfortable with the whole flying thing. Still, this would be my first real vacation in a long time, and finally I had enough money to pay for a nice one. So after swapping my purple jacket for some swim trunks, I found myself on a plane with some buddies heading off to a sun-drenched beach resort where I could kick back and recharge my batteries.

Among my fellow travelers on the plane that day was none other than Charo, the perennially popular guitarist, actress, and comedienne who's perhaps best known for her catchphrase "coochie-coochie." Charo's presence exposed a gap in my music education, because, I'll confess, I didn't really know who she was until my buddies informed me she was "that lady from *Love Boat.*"

Quickly, it began looking like my buddies and I should have taken the Love Boat because in midflight the pilot came on the PA to inform us he was going to have to work on some maneuvers over the Gulf. I turned my head and there was Charo fingering her rosary. Watching her, I wondered if I should be getting ready to kiss my own sweet coochie-coochie goodbye. I also remember thinking it was a real bitch that I was going to plunge into the Gulf without getting to make the album first.

From what I could gather, our plane basically had no flaps and had to land on one of the shortest runways in the world. When we finally landed, I recall our pilot slamming on the brakes and yelling "Whoa, Nelly"—which *aren't* words you ever want to hear coming from the cockpit. In the end, however, that wild flight wasn't my big Lynyrd Skynyrd–like stage exit—only a memorable bumpy ride, which at that point I'd gotten pretty used to.

Having survived my brief vacation, I went back to Los Angeles and immersed myself in the even more exciting business of recording my album. To borrow a phrase from Booker T.

and the MGs, time was tight. My record company was politely but loudly breathing down my neck about wanting to release the album in time for it to be a stocking stuffer. I didn't want to rush the process at all, but when a legend like my label boss, Clive Davis, wants something, it's hard to argue. Being as hardheaded as I am, I did argue a little anyway, knowing full well I'd lose.

Given the deadlines, I had my work cut out for me, but I use the word *work* reluctantly here, because the truth is, I would have *paid* to make my music. In fact, I *have* paid for that privilege more than once. Regarding those two independent albums I made, you should remember that such independence comes with a price tag. I paid to make those albums because no one else was asking. That's called making your own opportunities, and financing them too.

I had at most six weeks to make the album of a lifetime. Fortunately—with serious pressure mounting to deliver the goods—I found myself partnered with an excellent producer. Matt Serletic is a young, talented guy whose impressive resume includes lots of popular work with Matchbox 20 as well as a solo album by Matchbox 20's Rob Thomas. Matt has also worked with such music legends as Santana, Willie Nelson, and Aerosmith. But, of course, you don't work with a resume—you work with a person. Like so much else in life, making music usually comes down to chemistry.

Fortunately, right from the start Matt and I hit it off creatively. We found ourselves finishing each other's sentences, and more important, we found we were actually finishing the album on schedule, both a minor miracle and a big relief.

Making that album has probably been the happiest time of my life so far. Creating my own album from the ground up with Matt was an unbelievably satisfying experience. This was the fulfillment of all my dreams—much more than just winning a competition, even a *very* big one, on TV. For me, making that album was like finally getting my shot to play major-league ball, as opposed to just the ego stroke of going high in the draft.

It was the best feeling, driving to Matt's recording studio in the suburbs of L.A. with a reasonable expectation there were people somewhere in the world who'd want to *hear* what we were doing there. I've always thought of myself as a crowd-pleaser, and now at long last it looked like I might actually have a crowd to please.

We worked hard and we worked fast. When we weren't in the studio recording, I was out in the lounge listening to songs or writing with different songwriters. The only real breaks in the recording action came when I'd step outside and sit for a few minutes on an old ratty couch in the studio parking lot.

Inevitably, some kids from a nearby school would walk by and do a double take at me sitting there. Many is the time one of the kids would come up and say, "Hey, man, do people ever say you look *just* like Taylor Hicks?" And many is the time I'd reply, "Yeah, you know, it's funny, I get that *all* the time."

Despite the exhausting pace I was setting, I never felt more in tune with the universe. One of the lessons I've learned is that happiness isn't about fame or wealth—as nice as both can be. God knows we've all come across rich and famous people who find new and highly imaginative ways to make themselves unhappy.

To me, it seems like happiness is more about doing what you love and doing it well—and maybe even doing it in a way that will bring others joy or solace too. From what I've seen, being rich and famous can be thrilling, but it also strikes me as an unnatural and potentially unhealthy state. Ultimately, I think it's much more important that one's work is personally meaningful.

In mulling over what kind of songs to put on the album, I decided I wanted to make an album for everyone. I didn't want to target just one demographic. We *all* cope with similar pleasures and pains, core human emotions. I figured that if I dealt with those universals, everyone would feel the album was for them—provided, of course, that I sang the songs with emotional authenticity. That's probably the essence of what I learned from listening to Ray Charles: it all comes down to a singer connecting with a song.

The result was very much a collaborative effort, as it should be. I got to record some of my original songs, and I was lucky enough to have some of the world's best songwriters send me their songs for consideration. Other great songwriters actually agreed to write with me. Then there were all the talented musicians who agreed to contribute their playing. The foundation of the album is totally live, and Matt and I just built up everything from there, part by part, piece by piece, song by song.

It takes a village to make an album, and yet I made certain that each thread that was woven into the whole was something I felt good about. Sure, at times I had to give a little in terms of commercial considerations and radio formats, but the bones of songs I love are there, giving a solid structure to the whole effort. Now that I think of it, maybe I should have put a little message at the end saying, "I'm Taylor Hicks, and I approve this album."

Recording the album was very different from recording the single "Do I Make You Proud?" for *American Idol* because these were songs I wanted to record, not something I *had* to record. I still feel connected with that song, but this album really felt more meaningful. It really *did* make me feel proud.

One song on the album that I wrote myself means a whole lot to me. It's called "Soul Thing," and if you listen closely to it, you'll discover that it incorporates everything I've been doing with my life. "Soul Thing" is my story. For me, music is maybe our highest form of communication—it permits the telling of stories and the sharing of them with anyone who might want to hear them or even *need* to hear them.

There's a line in "Soul Thing" that says, "The road can be your friend, or the devil in disguise." To me, that sentiment rings all too true. Read the life stories of your musical heroes and you'll see that, regardless of what vehicle they chose to get around in, the road could be heaven or it could be hell.

"Soul Thing" hits home for me because it's so much about who I am and what I do. I'm proud that my name has become so closely associated with the word *soul*. The moniker used to describe people who dig what I do, the Soul Patrol, seemed to just take on a life of its own. I love that my supporters wound up naming themselves and did such a fine job of it. It's mind-blowing that my music caused a kind of community to form. I'd love to see the Soul Patrol stay together and mix with all sorts of other music lovers. Ideally, there should be no defending of territory going on among Jimmy Buffett's Parrotheads, or the Deadheads, or my own funky Soul Patrol. It's all good, so why be rival gangs when we can all be part of the same big party?

The opening track on the album that we titled simply *Taylor Hicks* is called "The Runaround." For me, that song is a new spin on all sorts of classic sounds. I also loved its title because in years past you could "Mess Around" with Brother Ray or "Shop Around" with Smokey Robinson and the Miracles, but now you could finally "Runaround" with Taylor Hicks. That song's got a great stride piano feel and it brings in an old New Orleans beat, but it's also very of the moment. Like so much of the music I love, it brings together the old and the new.

As I mentioned before, some dazzlingly talented artists sent in songs of theirs for me to consider recording. Bryan

227

Adams submitted a great soul ballad called "The Right Place," which I recorded, while Rob Thomas of Matchbox 20 fame offered a pretty song I just had to cut called "Dream Myself Awake."

That all-star help notwithstanding, my album *isn't* one of those records jam-packed with duets and special guest appearances. I decided to debut with a real Taylor Hicks album because I realized I needed to prove myself—not as "that *American Idol* guy," but as a real artist. I just didn't think it was smart to try to buy credibility by surrounding myself with lots of famous names. My hope now was to go out there and spread the word. Whatever happened, though, I already felt like a big winner.

While I was recording my album at Matt's studio, the little gas station right next door just happened to sell a lottery ticket that won somebody $45 million. That's a good trip to the gas station! Still, as I sat there living out my life's dream, I never doubted I was, in fact, the biggest winner around. As I've already said, yes, money's great, but getting to do exactly what you're meant to do, what you most *love* to do—that's the biggest win of all.

13
THE RIGHT PLACE

IF IT'S LOVING THAT YOU WANT,

WELL, IT'S LOVING YOU'LL RECEIVE

'CAUSE YOU'VE COME TO THE RIGHT PLACE, BABY.

—"The Right Place" by Bryan Adams and Jim Vallance

Usually, it's a long, strange trip from zero to hero. Thanks to the impact of *American Idol,* I was able to take the express train—and that's only made the journey seem all the more surreal.

Getting so famous so fast can be a scary and disorienting thing. As I was surfing the Internet one day I found out just how scary—I discovered that somehow I'd become a popular new Halloween costume. According to the article I read at AOL City Guide, here's all you really needed to become me:

A hideous jacket (purple works best here)
Harmonica
Baby powder dumped on head
A lazy bottom lip

And just for the sake of completeness, here's what the article listed as optional additions:

Random convulsions and "Whoo! Soul Patrol" yelps.

The other costumes the article helpfully suggested included ones based on Oprah, Paris Hilton, and Dick Cheney. How's that for entertaining holiday company? I did give some thought to trick-or-treating as Oprah this past Halloween, but it turned out I had the costume for Taylor Hicks lying around the house, so I figured, *What the hell—why not be myself?* Actually, I'm a great believer in just being yourself—it's easier *and* it's cheaper.

Getting famous was strange enough, but there are reverberations of fame that take some getting used to. For example, people can make headlines simply for not liking you, such as when Justin Timberlake was quoted as going after me. I have absolutely no problem with Justin Timberlake. I think it's sort of funny that people waste time imagining a feud between the two of us—but I studied journalism in school long enough to understand how these things work. Oh, well, I guess what doesn't kill me just makes me more famous.

It's important to be able to laugh at yourself, because you can be damn sure other people are already laughing somewhere. As somebody who's enjoyed *Saturday Night Live* for years, I was greatly amused to watch one of the cast members make fun of me one night. And I'll take as a compliment the fact that the great "Weird Al" Yankovic—a guy I grew up listening to on the radio and watching on MTV—has recorded a version of "Do I Make You Proud?" called "Do I Creep You Out?" Frankly, if that were the only song I'd ever heard me sing, I might creep myself out a bit too.

Finding yourself in the public eye, however, is not all laughs. It can sometimes by quite serious and moving.

For instance, I've heard stories that have taken my breath away because they've been so heartfelt. One sweet lady told me she was being beaten regularly by her husband, and that somehow listening to my music helped give her the strength to finally leave the bastard.

I'll always treasure an e-mail that I received from a family whose son had been very sick and on a ventilator. They explained that their boy saw me on *American Idol* and decided that, more than anything in the world, he wanted to learn how to play the harmonica. So this kid started playing, just as I once did, and slowly but surely his lungs and his muscles became stronger and stronger until finally he got off that ventilator. As hokey as it may sound, I wholeheartedly believe that music is a healing force for a lot of people, physically and spiritually. I know for a fact that Mother Music has been a source of strength for me.

There's a lesson here not just for people who end up on TV but for anyone who performs a role in other people's lives. That lesson? *You don't have to take yourself seriously, but always take what you do seriously.* You never know exactly how your actions might be impacting others.

These days with all the technological marvels that make it possible for people to cocoon themselves and veil their thoughts, dreams, and fears from others, a hand extended in gratitude—in the form of an e-mail, a letter, or a phone call—is something that should be cherished. I may not know the hundreds of people who write me and tell me I've touched their lives, but I certainly know where they're coming from. And in letting me know what I've meant to them, they've touched my life right back.

Let there be no doubt, it's good to be an Idol. Becoming an American Idol has its privileges. Let me now count some of the ways it's been a blast to be accorded this honor:

First, my exposure on *American Idol* has allowed me to share the stage with many music legends, including some who've been real heroes to me. For example, I got to sit in with Willie Nelson when he played the Red Rocks Amphitheater and perform with him "Will the Circle Be Unbroken." It was awesome, singing with one of music's greatest outlaws—and amusing, looking down and realizing that Willie wears New Balance sneakers just like I do. At heart, Willie and I are both modern-day Gypsies. Of course, Willie does his traveling in far higher style. As to whether I got to spend any quality time on Willie's famed tour bus—and all that implies—I hereby take the Fifth.

I was also thrilled to get the chance to jam with Widespread Panic—one of the bands my old college band Passing Through used to cover all the time. I was backstage hanging out at the Wiltern Theater in Los Angeles before one of Panic's shows when I let the band know I happened to have my harp with me. Taking my less than subtle hint, the guys generously invited me onstage to play "Fishwater" with them. As soon as I got offstage, I called up some of my old jam band buddies to brag shamelessly.

To my great amazement, I even got the chance to sit in with the most respected southern band of all, the mother of all jam bands, the Allman Brothers Band, when they played a show in Birmingham. It turns out that Gregg Allman is a big fan of *American Idol*—go figure. As a result, I was invited to take the stage in my hometown and play "One Way Out" with that storied group. I may very well have peed my pants while doing it, but I somehow managed to play a decent harp solo, if I do say so myself.

Most of the time, however, I was focused on making my own music. With a lot of help from Matt Serletic and the team in the studio, I was able to get my album finished and ready for its release on December 12, 2006. We shot the album cover at the famed Continental Club in Austin, Texas—an exceptionally cool joint with a red velvet stage where Stevie Ray Vaughan once ruled. After spending too much time hanging in big, antiseptic arenas, it was a pleasure to take a moment to breathe in some of that old club funk again. In fact, I think the air in there cleared my sinuses.

For a while, prior to the album's release, I'd been calling my strange blend of sounds "modern whomp." And I seriously considered calling the album *Modern Whomp* as a tribute to one of the greatest Ray Charles albums of all time—*Modern Sounds in Country and Western Music.* Ultimately, though, I decided to simply name the album after what I was really selling now—*Taylor Hicks.*

Then just when it seemed as if the rest of the world were going on an extended Christmas vacation, I hit the road and the airwaves to promote it. For a few weeks there, I was popping up all over the place on TV. I became a sort of all-purpose crooner, doing everything from singing a duet with the great Gladys Knight during halftime at the Orange Bowl to singing Christmas carols during the big tree-lighting ceremony in Rockefeller Center. At the latter event, I performed a version of "White Christmas" that was as off-white as I could possibly make it.

Helped by this last-minute push right before the holiday gift-giving season, the *Taylor Hicks* album got off to a very solid start, debuting at number two on the *Billboard* album charts. However, all of the sales numbers and chart placements I heard about seemed much less real and meaningful than one brilliant moment that will stay with me: on the release date, I walked into a record store in Times Square, and for the very first time, saw my brand-new major-label album on display *everywhere.* I thought back to those not-so-distant days when I couldn't even place a single copy of my old records at the Coconuts record store in Birmingham. No matter how many copies of *Taylor Hicks* I ultimately sold, I already felt a sense of triumph.

It was gratifying that the reviews for the album were mostly positive, and that within a week or so my record went gold. I did my best to promote *Taylor Hicks*—and by extension Taylor Hicks—wherever I possibly could. I even went on the Fox News Channel and did a little break dancing—and yes, for the record, even at age thirty, I can still do a pretty mean backspin.

Despite all the good news, the songs from my album weren't having a particularly easy time on the radio so far. Not for the first time, I encountered resistance from people who were quick to question where exactly I fit in—if I fit anywhere at all. After I performed "The Runaround" on television a number of times in December, we finally got around to putting out our first single in January 2007—"Just to Feel That Way," a very pretty ballad that nearly didn't make the album.

At this point in my life and career, any remaining negative voices don't bother me much. Hell, I've personally faced down Simon Cowell for months at a time, so who else out there can scare me? Ultimately, music is all about the people you can connect with—not those with whom you can't. At heart, I'm an entertainer at least as much as I'm a recording artist, and now, at long last, I was heading out on my very own tour.

But before my tour kicked off at the end of February, I had to make a very special trip first, journeying to New Orleans for a few days to serve as the grand marshal for the big Krewe of Endymion's parade during that great city's Mardi Gras celebrations. The whole experience was, of course, completely wild, especially for someone like me who'd never been able to even attend Mardi Gras, much less be a part of the action.

For perhaps obvious reasons, some of my memories of that weekend are a little hazy. I do remember tossing beads to fifty thousand people who were lined up forty deep for three and a half miles. I also remember getting hit hard in the face with beads at one point, and showing rare restraint in not jumping into the crowd and starting a fight. At another point in the parade, I actually had the mayor of New Orleans, Ray Nagin, quote Snoop Dogg at me, telling me to "drop it like it's hot." Trying to obey the mayor's orders, I ended up humping the side of my Mardi Gras float as the tuba player nearby played a cool bass line. It was at that exact moment that I realized the enormous journey I'd taken over the past year and a half.

For all the wonderful insanity of Mardi Gras, it was also inspiring to come back to this town, where my life seemed to change so dramatically, and see signs of renewal. It also meant a lot that I was able to get a little time to eat—and, yes, drink—with my friends Tracy and Brian Grubb, the couple who'd been married that fateful weekend when so much seemed to change.

Finally, since I was after all a player in perhaps the greatest music city on earth, I was honored to sit in with some of the city's finest musicians—Ivan Neville, Art Neville, George Porter Jr., and David Russell Baptiste—during a gig at a club called the Howlin' Wolf. All in all, my first Mardi Gras was nice work if you can get it, and for the time being, at least, I could.

At the end of February, the time had come to start my own nationwide tour. We began close to home in some of the beautiful old theaters and bigger clubs across the South, and it's my fervent hope that this tour doesn't really end until the day I die. The thing is, this was much more than just my latest road trip or an important chance to promote my album. This was, at long last, my best shot to build the kind of show of which I've always dreamed. To back me for this tour, I pulled together a tight and tasty eight-piece band including Brian Less from the Little Memphis Blues Orchestra on organ. My goal was to assemble a mix of talents that left enough room for the kind of soulful spontaneity that's always at the heart of the music I love. And just to assure you, the guys in the band—and our very own female vocalist—weren't the only ones working hard in rehearsals. I wrote down all my lyrics on posterboards and studied them closely to get myself absolutely ready.

In the midst of all this, I began putting together a set list that was almost like one of those great old Grateful Dead sets—a loose and ever-changing lineup, only a little shorter, since I don't yet have a similarly deep body of work. Eventually, I settled most nights on playing about three-quarters of the songs on the *Taylor Hicks* album, with a tendency to feature all the songs I wrote, including "Soul Thing," "The Deal," and "Hell of a Day," the last being another old fan favorite that we added to *Taylor Hicks* as an exclusive bonus track for Wal-Mart. To keep things fresh, we also worked up a version of all sorts of other material that we could play on a moment's notice—although I'm not sure the rest of the world really needed to hear our otherworldly version of "Knowing Me, Knowing You" by Abba.

Right from our first gig at the red-hot Coral Springs Center for the Arts in Coral Springs, Florida, on February 23, I felt I was in exactly the right place, to borrow the title from the song Bryan Adams gave me. I'd learned that Bryan and his longtime songwriter partner, Jim Vallance, originally wrote the song for Ray Charles himself, and I'm proud and thankful it eventually found its way to me.

As I stood on stage night after night, singing that song, "Soul Thing," "The Deal," "Just to Feel That Way," and so many others, I experienced the stunning sensation of being smack in the middle of a dream come true. After all those years of feeling slighted, ignored, or just flat-out rejected, I felt at peace with myself in a way I never had before.

Whether I'd ever become the world's biggest pop sensation was never the question, at least not for me. I simply wanted to sing for the people, and now I was doing just that—every night.

So far, the age of the audiences coming to my shows has stretched from eight to eighty, and I'm glad to welcome every one of them. I've seen firsthand that, regardless of age, everybody claps with the same wild enthusiasm. Every night after the show I get to meet some of the fans who gave me this chance of a lifetime, one vote at a time on *American Idol*. Some of them tell me their fingers still hurt from dialing so much on my behalf.

As if they haven't done enough for me already, some of the people who supported me so passionately during my *Idol* performances show up after the show with homemade brownies and other treats. I've sampled quite a few already, but I'm still keeping my weight down thanks to the rigors of the road. I bet I run five miles a night onstage, and that's the best workout plan I've ever found.

I've seen a lot of familiar faces at the shows and lots of old T-shirts on fans who were there even before *Idol*. One of the newer familiar faces in the crowd turned out to be Tina Wesson, who won *Survivor: The Australian Outback*. I felt her pain because sometimes being on *American Idol* was a little like being stranded on an island in the middle of nowhere, wondering which tree bug you were going to have to eat next. Recently, somebody told me that even Céline Dion is a fan of my music, and I'm hoping that I get to see her when our show travels to Las Vegas.

As our tour really got going, I became aware of some negative press regarding how the album was doing and speculation concerning whether I was keeping pace with other *American Idol* finalists over the years. In a way, it's the oldest story in the world: the same media that help make you are bound to turn on you eventually—at least a little. The honest truth is that at this point in my life, I've decided to stop trying to compete with anyone but myself. *American Idol* was a competition and I played it to win, but music is a way of life—at least, it is for me.

As I write these words, I've just played the House of Blues in Myrtle Beach, South Carolina, where we kicked things off with "Hell of a Day," "The Maze" from my new album, "Going Mobile" by the Who, and my new personal anthem, "The Right Place." In every new town we hit, I continue to feel like I'm in the right place. A couple of days ago, I played the Mobile Civic Center in Mobile, Alabama, and was happy to see that my grandmother Jonie turned up for the show. Like so many other people, she had some popcorn, a few beers, and, I'm told, a great old time.

In the next week or so, I'll be back in Nashville, Tennessee, the same town where I swung and missed so completely all those years ago when I was just starting out. That last time,

I stood outside the legendary Ryman Auditorium feeling totally lost. This time, I'm proud to say, I'll be *inside,* playing onstage as a headlining act and actually getting paid for it. From there, it's on to other cities, including Birmingham, Alabama. You could call that my hometown gig, but at least for me, they all feel like hometown gigs now.

WHAT'D I SAY?

I 've talked quite a lot about music in this book, and I hope you don't mind. For the record, I consider music my first language, with English coming in a distant second most of the time. So before we all head off in opposite directions for a while, I'd like to share whatever common sense I have with the help of some great music I've loved.

I've decided to do that by talking about ten recordings that have great meaning for me. None are my songs, so I don't profit in any way if you pick them up. Still, I hope you'll check out these songs or revisit them because I believe they can be quite useful in helping you on your way.

If you're a downloader, download them. If you continue to haunt record stores like I do, get shopping. And if you already know and love these songs by heart, then sing 'em to yourself as loudly and as frequently as possible to keep yourself moving in the right direction. If the people around you tell you that you can't sing, you can remind them that people told *me* the exact same thing, and most of those people are singing a whole different tune now.

Without further ado, here are the songs:

1. "RESPECT YOURSELF" — The Staples Singers

You've *got* to respect yourself if you ever want others to respect you. Believing in yourself can be highly infectious. Who knows—maybe you'll even start a whole movement of people digging you, just like I somehow did with the Soul Patrol. You can tell that the great Mavis Staples knew what she was singing about here. Even when I couldn't get respect from anybody else, I believed my music was good enough to be bought and sold. Not a lot of people purchased my early records. Yet for a guy coming up, it was a way of showing the world that I respected myself even if nobody else did.

Respecting myself saved me from destroying myself. It also helped me trust that I'd eventually make it big when that was very much a minority opinion. The same can happen for you, but only if you believe it. Remember, no one was lining up to get in business with me either, so I made a product and sold it myself. I had faith that what I did had value. For the vast majority of us, success is not something that's just going to happen. It's something we've got to *make* happen. So go ahead and make it happen.

2 "WORK TO DO"—The Isley Brothers

People, we all have work to do, so it's best that we get right down to it. And if you're going to get down, why not do it to the Isley Brothers?

Whatever else I learned as a kid, my father and my grandmother—two of the most important people in my life—taught me a lot about the importance and the dignity of hard work. I worry that kids today might think getting ahead is all about getting on TV and getting rich—as opposed to working hard and making their own way. Working hard has its own rewards. It sets you apart and gives you an edge. As the great quarterback Roger Staubach once put it, "There are no traffic jams along the extra mile."

To me, 50 percent of our job in this world is just getting up in the morning. If you make even that minimal effort, you're ahead of some folks. And if you get up in the morning enough times, and follow that with an honest day's work, I believe something good is going to happen.

3 "YOU CAN'T ALWAYS GET WHAT YOU WANT"— The Rolling Stones

The Stones are maybe the coolest band of all time, and this is one of their coolest messages. For me the key takeaway is not in the title but in the lines that come right after that. Because the truth is even if you *don't* get what you want, if you do try sometime, you really might find that you get what you *need.*

The point here for me is that even though life throws some tough breaks at you, there always remains that golden chance to make things better, but only if you keep trying.

Don't stay home in bed waiting for somebody to come knock on your door to deliver your big break. Nobody is going door-to-door to see if they can make you into the next great singer, the next great painter, or the next great CEO. Ultimately, it's not incumbent on anybody else to get you what you need—it's on you. So try sometime. Don't just wait for that magic wand to gently touch down on your shoulder because you could be waiting a long, long time.

4 "FORTUNATE SON"—Creedence Clearwater Revival

Sure, some sons and daughters are more fortunate than others, but why not own who you are and where you come from rather than spend your life feeling bad about yourself?

I love the way John Fogerty sings his heart out on this song proclaiming that he "ain't no senator's son." To me, he sounds pissed off, but proud of who he is and sticking up for himself to anyone who'll listen. I ain't no senator's son either. In fact, I'm a dentist's son, and apart from the complimentary fillings, that was no free ride either. We are who we are, and we can try to rise above the challenges we face, or we can give up and feel sorry for ourselves.

Whatever it is that makes you feel unlucky, I say *use* it to drive you toward your goals. Make your own good fortune. A little righteous anger can help along the way. The lyrics to this song are tough and painful, but listen closely: the man singing it sounds bloodied but far from defeated. In the end, it's that defiance that moves the song forward. And whether you're a fortunate or unfortunate son, forward is the only direction that leads toward a better place.

5 "THINK"—Aretha Franklin

Now, this one is easier said than done, but I suggest we all learn a lesson from the Queen of Soul and think about what we're doing. Be aware especially of the mistakes we're making—usually the same damn ones over and over again.

In this life, it helps to be street-smart *and* school-smart. You can't just hire a smart lawyer or doctor to do your thinking for you and assume everything's okay. You have to educate yourself enough to know what they're doing. The more you know, the more dangerous you are. And the more dangerous you are, the less people are likely to screw you over.

So for those of you who are still trying to figure where school fits into your life, please do as I say and not as I've done. Do yourself a big favor and pursue your education the same way you'd pursue any other dream—do it with all your heart.

6 "TAKE THE LONG WAY HOME"—Supertramp

This was the very first song I played on the harmonica. It's a song that's wound up taking me on a long, strange trip—one I hope never ends. This song means so much to me in ways that are hard to explain. The whole idea of home is one that felt a little bit elusive to me growing up. For a lot of us, it can take a long time to find the way home, especially when your own home is pretty broken.

Even in my life now, that song and that title just ring so true for me. I feel like I've been taking the long way home most of my career. For many years there, I never really felt like I had much of a home because I lived like a rolling stone. That's not to be confused with living like a Rolling Stone— which actually sounds pretty good.

It's going to be nice to actually see my physical home someday when I finally get to settling down. Until then, I'm living and breathing "Take the Long Way Home" and backing myself up on harmonica all the way there.

For the time being, I think I still feel most at home onstage, making a connection with a room full of people through music.

My advice to you: make your home wherever you find the most happiness.

7 "HOLLYWOOD NIGHTS"— Bob Seger

This song by the great Bob Seger always reminds me not to be too distracted by shiny objects or shiny people, and there are a lot of both in Hollywood. Go ahead and change your life, but never forget where you come from and who you are.

During the past year, my life has changed all around me, but I like to think that I haven't changed all that much myself. You could ask anyone around me, I think, and they'd tell you I'm pretty much the same guy—that to quote that other Seger favorite, I'm still the same, perhaps to a fault.

I humbly suggest that you surround yourself with people who'll have your back but are still willing to call you on your own BS. I have a lot of people around me who are watching me and keeping me in check.

Many people who are drawn to show business seem to want to endlessly reinvent themselves. The problem is, sometimes after a reinvention they don't know who they are anymore. I've come to Hollywood to make my name, but I haven't gone to "Hollywood" and never plan on doing so. Fame shouldn't be a goal—fame should be a way to get to a goal.

Except for every Halloween, when you're all dressed up in your Taylor Hicks costume, I don't think you should ever run away from who you are. Rather, I think you should run toward whomever you want to be.

It's like they say—wherever you go, there you are.

8 "TELL IT LIKE IT IS"—Aaron Neville

Never argue with a Neville Brother, or with Brother Ray, who once put it even more bluntly with "Tell the Truth." I'm a firm believer in telling the truth, even when the truth hurts. Think of it this way: in the end, telling the truth is easier than keeping up with a bunch of lies. It's also good karma.

9 "INSTANT KARMA!"—John Lennon

I've always believed in karma, and I believe you have to do what you can to keep your karma wheel turning in the right direction. This doesn't mean being a saint, only that you should make a conscious effort to treat people the way you'd like to be treated.

Call me naive, but I believe that good things happen to good people who do good things. And I also believe bad things happen to bad people who do bad things. Eventually, karma will kick in, and payback can either be a blessing or a bitch.

To me, there's no question that there's a higher power. Having faith in yourself—and in something bigger than yourself—can be crucial. Faith and spirituality are an essential part of who we are. Before everything good happened for me, I was in the very gradual process of getting spiritually correct. It continues to be an ongoing project. I firmly believe that the more spiritually correct you can be, the better off you'll be.

Faith creates opportunity, and it creates the strength to keep going while you wait for that opportunity.

10 "I BELIEVE TO MY SOUL"—Ray Charles

This is the last selection in my Top 10, but it's the number one message I want you to take from my story. Believe in yourself. Believe to your soul. Be confident. As Joe Namath once said, "When you have confidence, you can have a lot of fun. And when you have fun, you can do amazing things."

If you believe in yourself, anything that comes your way—good, bad, or really ugly—can't knock you too far off track. Believing in yourself is the thing—sometimes the only thing—that will carry you through any situation.

It's amazing what you can achieve when you combine belief, hard work, dedication, and hustle. Belief may be the *most* important, because a show of self-belief causes others to believe in you. It forges allies.

It's not easy, I know, to tamp down doubt. For most of us, there are a million breaks that *don't* go our way before there's a big one that does. But think of my example, and know that if it can happen for *me,* it can happen for *you.*

But don't *wait* for it to happen. Success is not something that just happens of its own accord. Success is what you're going to make happen right now.

Acknowledgments

R-E-S-P-E-C-T

I'd like to thank everyone who was part of my story, especially my family and my friends.

I'd like to thank David Wild for helping me get my story down on paper with style and soul.

Thanks to Alan Nevins and everyone at The Firm for being not only my team but on my side.

And I'd like to thank our esteemed editor, Rick Horgan, for Crowning me and making this book everything it could be.

And finally, thanks to all of you out there for sharing my story so far. Now, with a heart full of soul, get right back to making yours.

Index

♫

257

Index

Index

Index

Index

♫

"I Believe to My Soul" (Charles), 252

"I Can't Stop Lovin' You" (Charles), 39, 87

Ike and Tina Turner Revue, 115

"I'll Get Along Somehow" (Tubb), 92

"In the Ghetto," 196

"In Your Time" (Hicks), 61, 71

In Your Time (Hicks), 80–81, 87

Ingram, James, 195

"Instant Karma" (Lennon), 252

Iratowns, 78

Isley Brothers, 247

♫

J Records, 9

Jackson, Randy, 5, 10, 171–173, 182

"Jailhouse Rock," 196

Jarreau, Al, 4

Jenkins, Johnny, 35

Joel, Billy, 110, 130

John, Elton, 110, 186

Jones, Mitch, 136

"Just Once," 195

"Just to Feel That Way," 237, 240

♫

Keb' Mo' (*see* Moore, Kevin)

Kelly, Taylor Brooke, 57

King, B. B., 75, 120

Knight, Gladys, 236

"Knowing Me, Knowing You," 240

Kodak Theater, Hollywood, 3, 4, 12

Kool and the Gang, 130

Kristofferson, Kris, 92, 166

♫

LaMontagne, Ray, 193

Las Vegas, Nevada, 164–174, 192

Lennon, John, 252

Less, Brian, 136, 239

"Levon" (John), 186, 198

"Life's Been Good," 149

Little Memphis Blues Orchestra, 214–215, 239

"Living for the City" (Wonder), 193, 198

"Long Way Home, The," 65

Los Angeles, California, 138–140, 177, 181, 187–188

"Lullaby," 139

Lunceford, Patrick, 104, 136

Lynyrd Skynyrd, 45, 59

Lythgoe, Nigel, 6, 170–171

♫

"Macon County Blues" (Hicks), 120

Manilow, Barry, 192, 200–201

Marsalis, Wynton, 141

Matchbox 20, 223, 228

"Maze, The," 242

McDonald, Michael, 187

Index

McGraw, Tim, 90, 91

McPhee, Katharine, 6–7, 182, 196, 206

"Me and Bobby McGee," 166

Meat Loaf, 4, 5

Mellencamp, John, 37

Mercury, Freddie, 194

"Mess Around," 227

Meters, the, 109

Miller, Glenn, 133

Minor, Ricky, 186, 196

Modern Sounds in Country and Western Music (Charles), 87, 236

Moore, Kevin (Keb' Mo'), 115, 140, 142–143, 194

Morrison, Van "The Man," 35, 38, 109

Mullins, Shawn, 139

"Mustang Sally" (Pickett), 76

"My Friend" (Hicks), 109

♪

Nagin, Ray, 238

Namath, Joe, 252–253

Nashville, Tennessee, 85–97, 138, 139, 242–243

Nelson, Willie, 92, 95, 141, 220, 234–235

Neville, Aaron, 251

Neville, Art, 239

Neville, Ivan, 239

New Orleans, Louisiana, 154–158, 238–239

"Not Fade Away," 193

♪

Ole Miss–Arkansas football game, 108, 109

"On Broadway," 80

"One Way Out," 235

♪

Parrotheads, the, 227

Passing Through band, 74–78, 80, 104, 107, 112, 235

Pearson, Jay, 148, 150–152

People magazine, 57, 208

Phish, 74

Pickett, Wilson, 76

"Play That Funky Music," 195

Poole, Chris, 74

Porter, George, Jr., 239

Presley, Elvis, 67, 196

Preston, Billy, 170, 197

Primus, 79

Prince, 4–5, 19

Prine, John, 140

♪

Queen, 194

♪

Randolph, Robert, 115

Ray Charles Marketing Group, 209

Redding, Otis, 34–37, 42, 195, 198

"Respect Yourself" (Staples Singers), 246

Rice, Condoleezza, 219–220
Richie, Lionel, 187, 213
"Right Place, The" (Adams and
     Vallance), 228, 229, 240, 242
Riley, Bob, 196
Robinson, Smokey, 227
Rolling Stones, 56, 193, 247
Romijn, Rebecca, 201
"Runaround, The," 227, 237
Ryman Auditorium, Nashville,
     92–93, 243

♫

Sam and Dave, 38
Santana, 220
Saturday Night Live, 232–233
Seacrest, Ryan, 4, 11, 195, 199
Seat of the Soul, The (Zukav), 150
Seger, Bob, 38, 179, 250–251
Serletic, Matt, 223–224, 226, 235
"Seven Spanish Angels," 95
"Shop Around," 227
Sinatra, Frank, 39, 133
"(Sittin' On) The Dock of the Bay,"
     34, 35
Sledge, Percy, 41
Sly and the Family Stone, 193
"Somehow" (Hicks), 80, 83
"Something" (Harrison), 195
"Son of a Carpenter" (Hicks), 80
Sony Nashville, 96
Soul Stirrers, 153
"Soul Thing" (Hicks), 31, 99, 137,
     226–227, 240
Sounds of Blackness, 182

Southwest Airlines, 158, 159, 164
Spinal Tap, 104
Spoonful James, 78
Springsteen, Bruce, 43, 197
Staples, Mavis, 246
Staples Singers, 246
Steely Dan, 35
Stevens, Cat, 71, 185
Stewart, Rod, 185, 186
Studdard, Ruben, 166
Supernaw, Doug, 77–78
Supertramp, 35, 43, 65, 249–250
"Swanee River Rock," 172
"Sweet Home Alabama," 45, 59,
     77

♫

"Take Me Home Country Roads"
     (Denver), 194
"Take the Long Way Home"
     (Supertramp), 43, 65, 249–250
"Takin' It to the Streets"
     (McDonald), 187
Taylor Hicks (album), 221–228,
     235–237, 240, 242
Taylor Hicks Band, 103–121,
     125–128, 135–138
"Tell It Like It Is" (Neville), 251
"Think" (Franklin), 249
Thomas, Rob, 220, 228
Thoreau, Henry David, 121
"Thrill Is Gone, The," 75
"Tighten Up," 80
Timberlake, Justin, 168, 232
Time magazine, 219